LIBERTY
FOR ALL

LIBERTY
FOR ALL

A MANIFESTO FOR RECLAIMING
FINANCIAL AND POLITICAL FREEDOM

RICK NEWMAN

palgrave
macmillan

First published in 2015 by PALGRAVE MACMILLAN® TRADE
in the United States—a division of St. Martin's Press LLC, 175 Fifth
Avenue, New York, NY 10010.

Palgrave® and Macmillan® are registered trademarks in the United States,
the United Kingdom, Europe and other countries.

ISBN: 978-1-137-27936-1

Library of Congress Cataloging-in-Publication Data

Newman, Rick, 1965–
    Liberty for all : a manifesto for reclaiming financial and political
freedom / Rick Newman.
 pages   cm
    ISBN 978-1-137-27936-1 (alk. paper)
    1. Liberty—United States. 2. American Dream. 3. Self-reliance—
United States. I. Title.
U241.N47   2015
323.440973—dc23

                                                            2014029035

Design by Letra Libre, Inc.

First edition: February 2015

10 9 8 7 6 5 4 3 2 1

Printed in the United States of America.

CONTENTS

LIBERTY
FOR ALL

ONE

FREEZING FOR FREEDOM

"YO, RICK! YOU BETTER GET OVER HERE!"

The moment before I heard this, an urgent summons was about the last thing I expected. In fact, there were 12 of us each ruing one of the slowest evenings of our lives. One was sick, enduring the woodsman's nightmare, trying to tough it out in a camping hammock strung between two trees, with a tarp cinched over it to keep the rain out. Two others were lost somewhere in the woods, or maybe they had retraced their steps and made it back to civilization. The rest of us were soggy and frigid and quietly dreading a night that was likely to be more miserable than any of us had prepared for.

An interlude of excitement should have been welcome, to get some blood pumping and take my mind off the creeping numbness. But when I turned around I realized Omar, the bulkiest member of our group, was stomping on something that on closer inspection turned out to be my only pair of gloves, the thin cotton gardening variety, which had become saturated after about five minutes of use and were wholly inadequate given the circumstances, and were now, on top of that, on fire.

Omar, a caustic, goateed Dominican American who might look like Bob Dylan if he lost 100 pounds, stomped like he was trying to kill a copperhead as I tried to figure out whether he was ruining my gloves or saving them. "Your gloves kinda burned up," he explained as I reached down to snatch the smoking pile of fabric from the ashen mud beneath his boot. "They're toast." This was alarming news since I was already underdressed and had been counting on those gloves to keep my fingers on life support until daylight, if it ever arrived.

Gloves had seemed like the last thing I would need as I began the "Tough Preppers' Bug-Out Weekend" in the Catskill Mountains, about 130 miles north of New York City. It was mid-September. The forecast called for dry, mild weather in the 60s, even in the mountains. No freak storms were on the way. As a novice prepper, I had spent the last month researching survival gear and stocking up, the main goal being not to look like an ass among hearty folk who might mistake me for a soft suburbanite. I had a Leatherman multitool and a flip-top water purification bottle and stormproof matches and a radio that doubled as a cell phone charger when I turned a crank and a bunch of other gizmos to help me simulate an escape from mayhem, all stuffed into a black "spec-ops tactical backpack" I purchased online. Gloves! I must have had 20 pairs at home, for skiing, shoveling snow, jogging in winter and even riding a motorcycle through the frost, from back when I had my second (or was it my third?) midlife crisis. But the only advice I had noticed about gloves was to bring some canvas or leather ones along, just in case work broke out.

My regular work gloves in the garage had seemed too dirty to stuff into my brand-new spec-ops tactical backpack, so I brought the gardening gloves—freshly laundered. And wouldn't you know it—work broke out right away. The bug-out weekend began gloriously, with a mountain hike to our campsite under warm blue skies that left our group sweating and gulping water within 10 minutes. We were all still sweating when we reached the campsite about an hour later, but the sun had slipped behind the mountaintop by then, and the woods surrounding our little encampment turned out to be damp as a bog once you stepped off the trail and began to tromp through the underbrush. There had been a thorough downpour the night before, and unlike the yard in front of my house, which had been completely dry by the following afternoon, the ground at the bottom of the woods was as wet as if the rain had just ended. It probably never really dries out down there.

We all brought our own gear—tent, sleeping bag, food, clothes and whatever bug-out gear you wanted to test on the trip. But there was one communal activity: building and sustaining a fire. I had tried to anticipate all sorts of eventualities I might want to be prepared for: a bear attack, drenching rain that soaked everything in my bag, getting hurt, getting lost, even getting mugged, since I was in the woods with a bunch of urban oddballs I didn't know. But it hadn't occurred to me that we'd have to fetch our own wood. I guess I figured the $5 fee for the trip included all the wood you could burn, delivered and stacked by the firewood fairy.

So the men in the group—or rather, most of them—set to work doing the one thing men still feel a primordial obligation to be good at: building a fire. First we had to gather wood, which wasn't exactly laying around in log form but was inconveniently buried beneath weeds, infested with bugs or tangled in vines. And all of it was wet.

Firewood duty immediately revealed who were the pros and who were the amateurs in the group. Jason, our lead prepper, was a burly New York City firefighter who had trekked up the mountain with an axe in one arm—not a folding, camper-style axelet, but the kind of bad-ass axe, as long as a baseball bat, that firemen use to crash through doors. That was in addition to the 75 pounds or so of gear on his back. I offered to carry it for a spell at one point, and he just glared at me, as if insulted. John, another practiced prepper, had a nifty folding tree saw that collapsed to the size of a ruler yet could cut through a 12-inch tree trunk in about a minute. Teli, a contractor from New Jersey, had a variety of blades and other tools that would probably allow him to build a house right there in the woods if necessary.

I had a two-inch blade on my little Leatherman that was capable of spreading cheese, cutting rope and perhaps killing a salamander if I got lost for days and desperate for food. As for wood, I might be able to whittle with it, but that wouldn't help much with the fire. Thus, I discovered the First Rule of Prepping: always make friends with people who have better gear than you do.

I wasn't there to prove myself a master prepper. I was there to find out if preppers knew anything important I didn't. I assumed some members of the group—okay, maybe the entire group—would have better outdoor survival skills than me. The question was whether that mattered. I was testing a new theory that Americans were coming up short on self-reliance at a time when they were going to need it a lot more than they realized. This wasn't the usual tirade about Americans going soft, morphing into pampered ninnies who don't know how to take care of themselves. That was part of it, but there have always been people who fit that description, relative to what's going on in society around them. America as a nation has almost always risen to a challenge because a critical mass of its people—far from everybody, but enough to pull the rest along—have mustered the grit and ingenuity needed to win or come back from defeat. There are surely still people like that today. But are there enough to pull the whole country out of a funk? Does America still sink or swim as one people with some sort of shared identity? Or has American society fragmented so much through globalization, the Internet, toxic politics or some other unprecedented force that that our collective self-healing properties have failed, and we're all on our own?

These aren't purely theoretical questions; they're tangible problems in many Americans' everyday lives. In my business as a financial journalist, we talk about the economy as if it's one overarching thing that affects everybody the same, like the weather in your hometown or the Super Bowl when everybody's watching. It's not. In the taxonomy of everyday economics, there are two big subdivisions: one in which people have the skills to get ahead, and another in which they don't. The pressure so many people feel these days is the grind of a tectonic shift between these two subdivisions. The first subdivision—let's call it Progressia—is a land of abundance, the way Currier & Ives might depict a wholesome society. There's plenty of everything in Progressia, except, perhaps, leisure time. The only real financial pressure is the kind people create, by imagining themselves as superheroes and trying to accomplish more than a mere mortal can. This subdivision is generally a pleasant place to live, but it's getting smaller because there's a mostly one-way flow of people into the other subdivision—more like Regressia—which is getting more crowded and contentious. Regressia is the subdivision in which people feel like they're falling behind, even when they work hard and play by the rules and do the things you were always supposed to do to succeed in America. A lot of people in this universe aren't succeeding, and it's not clear their prospects are going to improve any time soon. They might actually get worse as an unsettling wealth gap grows, especially if the government runs short of money at some point, which seems likely, and has no choice but to cut back on spending programs that disproportionately benefit this group.

I'm not an alarmist who feels class warfare will tear the country to shreds. But something profound has changed in America, and a good way to get to the bottom of it is to abide by the old journalistic adage: Follow the money. We are clinging to old norms regarding opportunity, prosperity and financial independence that no longer apply. As the following chapters will show (and many Americans already know), working hard no longer guarantees anything, except you'll be tired. No rule of nature declares that kids will automatically have better opportunities than their parents. The very idea of the American Dream has become ossified and distorted. Powerful external forces combined with self-imposed limitations are diminishing our financial freedom—our ability to get ahead if we choose to—which in turn impedes many other freedoms. The magic of a free-market society like we have in America is that it creates new wealth for most people when the rules are clear and people compete fairly. That's why there have been remarkable improvements in living standards for nearly everybody over time. When the system breaks down, however, it becomes more like a zero-sum confrontation in which some advance at the expense of others. That produces the kind of societal ruptures we see in the destructive political antics so many people are sick of, and the plain incivility citizens show each other in blue-red America.

A lot of people feel the system works against them these days, and the data is on their side.[1] There's heated debate among policy-makers about what to do as prosperity evades more and more people. But ordinary folks can't do much to change policies in Washington, and besides, waiting for better government policies isn't exactly the fast boat to riches. Sure, it matters a lot that we have good laws, effectively enforced, and government programs that help those who need it. But these things merely create opportunity; it's up to us to seize it. With media everywhere these days—including literally in our pockets and purses via the smartphones we all carry—we focus way too much on the usually dispiriting news about politics, and way too little on what we can all do on our own to make our lives better. We seem to talk more than ever about freedom as we make choices that sacrifice the same freedom we supposedly crave. We gripe about a lousy economy while shackling ourselves with debt and making our own prosperity somebody else's responsibility, like the boss's or the president's. We condemn craven politicians while allowing them to manipulate us with cynical half-truths we can't be bothered to check out. And just as we face the increasing need to muster personal freedom and the resourcefulness that comes with it, many of us are discovering we don't know how.

I was out there in the woods, damp and freezing, to test the extent of my own freedom and see if I was optimizing my own prosperity. And I was lacking anything resembling a saw, which you need to cut firewood, which you need to keep warm when it's cold, which may ultimately determine whether you survive. To compensate for this embarrassing deficit, I decided I was probably more of a gatherer than a lumberjack. I scrambled into the woods and began to claw at anything that looked like it might burn, the bigger the better. I hauled tree limbs and even a couple of toppled trunks back to the campsite, where the cutting crew took turns sawing. I wasn't the Alpha Prepper, but I wasn't the slacker of the group, either. A few others seemed content to hang around the campsite, ask questions and avoid anything that might cause blisters. Omar, meanwhile, had plenty of commentary to offer on the correct manner of cutting wood and the proper way to vent a fire, but he seemed averse to demonstrating how.

Since everything in the woods was wet, my cotton gloves were soaked by the time I pulled my first branch back to camp. By that time, it was starting to get dark. Then it began to drizzle. Then the temperature dropped, and the sunny start to the day suddenly seemed like a memory trick. We had somehow been teleported to some frigid region of the globe where you really did need to prepare for disaster. There was one consolation: the fire. The collective effort of half a dozen determined men finally coaxed the wet timber into a reluctant burn, and we all inched closer and closer to the flames as it got colder and wetter and every one of us tried to delay the inevitable, unhappy duty of retiring to a solitary plastic tent.

I placed my soggy gloves on one of the rocks framing the fire pit. I'd need them during the night, and it was hot on the rock, and I figured they'd dry quickly. It didn't happen quickly enough, however, so I pushed them closer to the fire and walked a few steps over to where I had assembled my tent and started to organize my stuff for the night. That's when Omar bellowed to me. Once I finally pulled my smoldering gloves from beneath his feet, I grabbed some water from my tent and wetted them down all over again. Once the last spark was doused, I could see that the part that had burned was mostly the cuff on one glove, where it went over the wrist. The fingers were still intact, and the other glove was muddy but mostly unburned except for a couple of pinholes caused by sparks. If I had found these shabby-looking gloves in my garage, I would have thrown them away in an instant. But I treasured them now. My fingers were already losing sensation, even jammed into my pockets, and that mildly molten fabric might be the last barrier preventing frostbite. All I needed to do was dry them off. So I placed them on the rock near the fire once again, and didn't take my eyes off them until they were as toasty as if they had just come out of the dryer. When I finally retreated to my dreary little tent, it was with 10 fingers I could feel.

TWO

THE LIBERTY TRAP

A YEAR EARLIER, I DIDN'T EVEN KNOW WHAT A PREP-per was. But I knew something was going sour in American society. People were disgusted. Their outrage took many different forms— Tea Partiers eager to shut down the government, protesters on Wall Street trying to shut down the banks, taxpayers pissed off at the nanny state, the underprivileged resentful of the wealthy. There has always been tension in American society, but it usually blends with optimism and on balance produces progress. That optimism seemed to be in retreat. America had become a crabby country. In nearly every corner, the nation seemed to be increasingly populated by people falling behind, placing blame, waiting for help and losing their nerve.

There are all kinds of socioeconomic news threads that compete for our attention, from the glorification of celebrities to the disruptive power of digital technology to the political polarization of the entire electorate. But one ubertrend connects nearly all of them: sustained stress on the middle class and a measurable decline in overall living standards. Compared with most other countries, America remains a place of enviable prosperity. US GDP per capita is still the highest of any large country, with only small, homogenous nations such as Qatar, Luxembourg and Denmark, plus Canada and Australia, doing better.[1] Many foreigners continue to regard America as the world's most desirable place to live. And even in the midst of a global economic slowdown that started on Wall Street in 2008, the United States emerged as the most resilient of the big, powerhouse economies. But compared with itself—10, 20 or 30 years ago—America seems shabby and shaken, like an aristocrat whose funds are running dry and who's getting calls from a collection agency for the first time ever.

Beginning around 1980, subtle changes began to occur in the US economy that would ultimately become the making of a crisis. US companies began shifting work out of the United States. Large portions of Europe and Asia began to compete effectively with the United States after a long period of recovery from the ravages of World War II. By the 1990s, China and other developing nations were emerging from the gloomy shroud of hard-core communism and beginning to taste the pleasures capitalism can bring. Back in the United States, the value of certain uncommon skills—math and science proficiency, technical knowledge and, of course, computer programming—began to climb as the value of a high school diploma and plain old hard work declined. Consumers got more accustomed to using debt to finance purchases. More women entered the workforce and enrolled in college, while men's pay and skill levels tended to stagnate.

For a long time, America was such a colossal wealth-generating machine that many of these changes went unnoticed or simply failed to generate much concern. If there is such a thing as peak prosperity, it probably occurred in the late 1990s, when US economic strength was still near its zenith and opportunity was expanding for women, minorities, the underprivileged and others who didn't participate so much in the Waspy revels of the 1950s and 1960s. But by the 2000s, Americans had finally racked up too much debt, fallen too far behind in the global workplace and become too complacent about their presumed right to enjoy the good life. The corrective mechanisms were a brutal housing bust, a financial collapse and a near-depression, which left the middle class in the crater it's trying to climb out of today. The best evidence of this backsliding is median household income, which, adjusted for inflation, is about 7 percent lower than it was at the beginning of the twenty-first century—the deepest and most sustained drop in living standards since the 1930s.[2] At the same time, the incomes of the top 1 percent of earners have been soaring, with the gap between the rich and the rest the largest it has been since the party days right before the Great Depression hit.[3] And it's not necessarily over.

These troubling economic trends have generated the dominant media narrative of our time: Somebody is screwing you over. You'll recognize the familiar storylines: The rich are getting richer at the expense of everyone else. The government is a voracious beast that devours the hard-earned income of taxpayers who ought to be free to spend their money themselves. Working hard benefits the boss but not the worker, while Joe Six-Pack has become expendable. Eventually, most companies will consist of nothing more than a few rich executives and a bunch of robots and computers.

There's plenty of legitimate evidence that it's getting harder for most people to get ahead. But a vital part of the story has been missing:

Maybe you and I are doing something to screw ourselves over. Maybe the misfortunes of the middle class aren't entirely somebody else's fault. Maybe too many Americans are limiting their own prospects. Maybe self-reliance and self-determination are just as important as they've always been, regardless of all the modern inventions meant to make life easier and success automatic. And maybe Americans gained so much freedom during the last several decades that they didn't even notice when they started to forfeit their very own freedom. This is something I have come to regard as the Liberty Trap: a place where false presumptions of freedom diminish actual freedom. We have gotten so used to the idea we are entitled to prosperity and opportunity that we have stopped looking for it; we simply expect it to arrive. The Liberty Trap entices us by evoking the privileges of the past, when success for many was abnormally easy. It's a trap because it persuades us things should always be the way they used to be, dulling our instincts for adaptation. You get stuck in the Liberty Trap when you give lip service to liberty without actually cultivating it, and freedoms mistakenly assumed to have been granted in perpetuity dissipate through neglect. America may be a nation founded by freedom fighters, but it is in danger of becoming a nation of freedom forfeiters.

One well-known problem is the unprecedented number of people dependent upon government assistance, from food stamps to unemployment aid to aptly named entitlement programs such as Medicare, Medicaid and Social Security. This is the nanny state conservatives often decry. They shouldn't be so smug, however. They're probably right about an entitlement mentality that's become too pervasive, about too many people expecting a handout from too few people paying taxes. But something even more pernicious is going on: People are exercising the freedom to give up their freedom, and not even re-alizing it. And this is happening throughout the middle class, which is why the Liberty Trap has become an under-recognized national problem.

Since this book focuses on liberty and freedom, it's important to explain what these two highly charged words mean in terms of to-day's economic and political trends. Chapter Five includes a brisk and no doubt captivating review of how these concepts have changed over time. Sneak peak: What the ancient Greeks or America's founding fathers considered freedom is quite different from the way we think of it today. To some extent, the words *liberty* and *freedom* are synony-mous, and in many cases I've treated them that way. Yet there are subtle differences. *Liberty* connotes an overarching status in which there are no unusual impediments to the expression of self. *Freedoms* tend to be more specific—freedom of religion, freedom of speech, freedom of assembly and so on. It's worth keeping in mind that these are Western and in some cases peculiarly American ways of thinking of these concepts, enshrined in seminal documents such as the Dec-laration of Independence and the US Constitution. I've updated these classic concepts of liberty and freedom in this way: Liberty is the abil-ity to make of your life what you wish, within reasonable constraints, while freedom represents access to the resources necessary to enjoy liberty. They're very closely related, yet marginally different—like air and oxygen, perhaps, or broth and soup. Most important, these words imply no political ideology whatsoever and must be understood to be impervious to partisan manipulation.

We all know about headline freedoms such as the right to own guns, look at porn, have an abortion, marry anybody you want or even secede from the Union, if you're Texas. These might be best characterized as political freedoms that depend upon decisions made by elected officials and the policymakers they appoint. Political freedoms are important, needless to say, which is why people get riled up about them. But there's another vital freedom that helps determine all the others, even though it gets less recognition: financial and economic freedom, which affects nearly everything about where you end up in life. The news is dominated by stories about political freedom, but the loss of financial and economic freedom is arguably the greater danger these days. The growing gap between rich and poor and the falling living standards of the middle class are de facto evidence Americans are losing their financial freedom.

One reason people get fighting mad over political freedoms is they're usually able to identify a villain who clearly represents a threat. If you're a gun-rights advocate, the enemy is the gun-control lobby trying to tighten laws restricting your right to own, carry and shoot a firearm. If you're an abortion-rights advocate, the enemy takes the form of activists working to ban abortion in state capitals and the protesters who try to intimidate women seeking procedures at abortion clinics. These disagreements pit people against people and become intensely personal, which is why they end up cast as epic battles for freedom. But who's the villain if you're a college grad who can't find a decent-paying job? Who's the villain if you're in your 40s or 50s and instead of enjoying your peak earning years, you endure one career setback after another? Who's the villain if you get laid off from a company that has no choice but to downsize because it faces ruthless competition from new firms with better technology?

When something threatens our financial freedom, there's usually not a ready-made foe we can easily pin the blame on. So we look for proxy villains and sometimes find them, in whichever political party happens to be in power at the time, or in some heartless business owner who really ought to do the right thing and lose money in order to keep people employed on his own dime. These are weak explanations that usually lead us off the trail, leaving us unsure about what's really going on and confused about where to target our frustration. Safeguarding our financial freedom should command as much of our mental energy as the defense of political freedom or any other freedom—maybe even more. But since the narrative is murky and the plot lines complex, our attention wanders. Taken to the extreme, people energized to defend their freedom in this way will end up with lifelong access to abortions and all they guns they want—but they'll be poor, frustrated and financially entrapped.

There's a lot of talk across the country about personal liberty and rugged individualism and getting the government out of our lives—especially during election season, when every politician who needs your vote suddenly has a new plan to safeguard freedom and save America. But the data shows Americans are becoming *more* dependent on the government and a lot of other big institutions, not less. For the most part, they're doing so willingly. In 1980, total federal spending on Social Security, Medicare, Medicaid and a variety of aid programs for the needy was 10.1 percent of the nation's GDP. That rose to 13.5 percent by 2014, and the Office of Management and Budget projects it will rise to 14 percent by 2019. An increase of a few percentage points might not seem like a lot, but since the US economy is so huge, the increase in spending from 1980 to 2014 adds up to nearly $1.2 trillion per year, in today's dollars, after adjusting for inflation.[4] That's a lot of extra money spent on entitlements. It's nearly twice the Pentagon's entire annual budget, and if divided among every American who filed a tax return, it would amount to about $8,800 per person.[5] Of course, Washington borrows part of that money every year instead of imposing the full cost on US taxpayers, which is why America's national debt totals a mind-boggling $18 trillion.[6] But imagine if Washington paid for everything on a cash basis as we went along, and imposed tax hikes averaging $8,800 on every taxpayer every year, just to cover current expenses. Voices might rise.

The government layered even more goodies on top of all those standing benefits in response to the Great Recession, which lasted from 2007 to 2009. Those benefits included aid for homeowners, home buyers, the unemployed and many others down on their luck, along with temporary tax cuts for literally everybody earning a paycheck. Yet as more money flowed out of Washington, the more resentful people seemed to get, as if they felt somebody else was getting a better deal at their expense. Then came the Patient Protection and Affordable Care Act—aka Obamacare—which is either a godsend or the end of civilization as we know it, depending on whom you ask. Obamacare was meant to address a large, debilitating problem: the lack of adequate health-care coverage for nearly one-sixth of the US population. Most developed nations have health-care systems similar to Obamacare—except they're even more centrally controlled by the government than the US system is, and they're far less controversial. In America, however, our suspicion of central planning is so profound that we practically sabotage what is meant to be helpful. That sort of wariness left Obamacare a legislative monstrosity from the outset, on account of workarounds and triple bank shots meant to preserve or mimic a free-market dynamic in the health-care system. The hodgepodge layering of public and private bureaucracies and the almost absurd complexity of the law that emerged was a self-inflicted fiasco—not just by Democrats who crafted and supported the law, but by everybody who had a hand in shaping it, including those who tried desperately to kill it. As a nation, America has the freedom to handicap itself, just as individuals possess the freedom to give up their freedom. Our elected officials in Washington have been adeptly exercising that perverse privilege.

The big political fight during the next decade or two is going to be over one basic thing: who should pay for all the bills the government has racked up. That is fundamentally an economic problem likely to affect the financial wherewithal of millions. Defenders of Social Security and Medicare argue with some justification that people in those programs are only getting back from the system what they put in. But most people who draw those benefits today, or will in the near future, are likely to get back considerably more than they contributed. The numbers vary by age, income, work history and other factors, but as one example, a couple both aged 70 today who lived on one average income before retiring will have paid about $361,000 in lifetime taxes for Social Security and Medicare. But they'll draw about $966,000 in benefits, adjusted for inflation, if they achieve an average life expectancy, according to the nonpartisan Urban Institute. In other words, those lucky retirees are getting back nearly three times what they contributed. The payback premium is smaller for retired couples who enjoyed a higher income or who both worked, but in each of six scenarios examined by the Urban Institute, retirees get back more than they paid in.[7] Many people who receive benefits intended for the needy, such as housing assistance, food aid, school lunches for kids and disability payments, pay even less into the system, and sometimes nothing, since that's the whole point of aid to the underprivileged.

Some people feel America would be better off if we showed welfare recipients some tough love and dialed back the benefits, for their own good. It's feeble logic, however, to blame the nation's big economic problems on deadbeats seeking a handout. That may fulfill a narrative some critics prefer, but it leaves out another big category of federal largesse that goes largely to the middle class and the wealthy. These "tax expenditures," as they're known, include subsidies, tax breaks and other giveaways that go to people with relatively high incomes, including the rich. Altogether they account for about 42 percent more in federal expenses each year than Social Security, which is the next biggest federal spending category. Most Americans may not be familiar with that wonky-sounding phrase—tax expenditures. But just about everybody who buys a home knows about the federal tax deduction for mortgage interest, which is worth thousands of dollars per year on a typical house. That's a huge subsidy for the 58 million American families with a mortgage, and most homeowners tend to be middle class or above. Other subsidies enjoyed by ordinary folks include the tax deductibility of employer-provided health insurance (which covers 150 million Americans)[8] and contributions to certain retirement plans such as 401(k) accounts (51 million Americans).[9] Then there's the capital gains tax, which is assessed on investment income at a much lower rate than regular income tax and primarily benefits the wealthy. These various perks are practically invisible to people who enjoy them because for the most part you don't have to do anything to get them other than declare your mortgage interest on your tax return. So we think of these as automatic givebacks the same way Social Security and Medicare recipients come to think of their benefits—as entitlements. We deserve them.

You might think we're all paying more in taxes, or at least somebody's paying more in taxes, to finance this lavish buffet of benefits. Nope. In fact, the federal tax burden has declined for virtually all taxpayers since 1979, according to the Congressional Budget Office, which, even though it's an arm of the least popular legislative body in global democracy, is reliably nonpartisan and regarded as one of the few honest brokers in Washington. Everybody tends to think federal taxes are too high, but when you account for all the loopholes and giveaways, they're actually low from a historical perspective—and extraordinarily low compared with all the benefits Washington doles out (thanks to the time bomb known as federal borrowing). The largest tax reductions since 1979 have accrued to the top 1 percent and the bottom 20 percent of earners—the rich and the poor, in other words. Everybody else's federal taxes have fallen by less, but still, they've fallen. Keep in mind, this doesn't account for state and local taxes, including property taxes, which can take a big bite out of income in some areas. Yet there's far more vitriol directed at the federal government, which takes a smaller bite out of paychecks than it used to, than at state and local governments that are more likely to have raised taxes.

There's nothing inherently wrong with any of our federal entitlement or benefit programs—as long as somebody pays for them. Ah ha! There's the missing link. We're borrowing to finance benefits that are expensive, and somebody is going to have to pay for them eventually. Defenders of Social Security and Medicare rightly argue that those programs are funded by a dedicated tax and bureaucrats can't arbitrarily decide to spend that money on other things. But when the pucker moment comes and the spending gap has to be closed, it's a safe bet Congress will change the law and the tax code based on who has the most lobbying sway at the time. Social Security and Medicare are cherished programs, but they're also the most expensive items in the federal budget, and they'll only get more costly as baby boomers begin to claim their unfair share. Somebody is going to get stuck with a very large bill when we can no longer borrow at rock-bottom rates to fund benefits taxpayers can't afford.

As a journalist covering the economy and the fortunes of the middle class, I see a future in which a lot of people are going to get cut off as we will inevitably have to rectify the mismatch because of the huge amount the government spends and the lesser sums it takes in. To keep supporting everybody with a finger in the public purse would require huge tax hikes in the future, which Americans seem unlikely to tolerate. Without major tax hikes, spending will have to be cut, and those cutbacks will hurt a lot more people than expected because government largesse has become more pervasive than most people realize.

Nobody knows exactly when the money will run short, but people who think about this problem (which isn't that many people to start with) tend to believe a huge economic crisis will announce itself at some point and we'll all know precisely when the Great American Reckoning has begun. But we should also consider the possibility that the reckoning will be subtle, chronic and pernicious. Crises tend to develop in ways the experts don't foresee—which is why they end up as crises—and blow in through the side door when everybody's focused on the front. The crisis, in fact, might already be here, spreading slowly like the weeds I never see in my backyard garden until one day they suddenly threaten to choke off everything. If we're not at the beginning of a crisis, how do we explain declining incomes, falling living standards and the worst jobless recovery since World War II? We've already been through a lost decade in which fewer people are getting ahead and more are falling behind. And if you're a conservative who wants to blame the liberal president, or a liberal who wants to blame the conservatives, pipe down, please: The lost decade transcends both political parties and shows clearly that economic distress is a nonpartisan phenom-enon. Presidents and their economic policies determine the well-being of the typical family much less than the blame or credit they get suggests. Meanwhile, the old economic models keep forecasting a robust recovery that ought to be right around the corner, yet keeps slipping out of sight like a new species whose footprints we've seen but whose actual existence we can't quite prove.[10]

Ordinary people, meanwhile, struggle to understand what to make of all this, with consumer behavior gradually changing in ways that might make the whole problem worse. Confusion and dismay over the scarcity of good jobs has forced the percentage of adult Americans who work or want to work to the lowest level since the late 1970s, before women began to flow into the workforce en masse. The labor force participation rate, as it's called, peaked in 2000 at around 67 percent. It's now around 63 percent. Again, a difference of a few percentage points might seem inconsequential, but that adds up to about 10 million adult Americans who would be in the labor force if the participation rate had remained steady. Instead, they've decided not to work for reasons that might be personal, economic or psychological. The participation rate for women has dipped by about three percentage points since it peaked. The drop for men has been more pronounced, falling by about twice as much as for women since 2000.[11] There are reasons: Men tend to work in blue-collar industries such as construction and manufacturing that have been hit hardest by the changing economy, while women are overrepresented in recession-resistant fields such as health care and education. Still, it's economically disastrous when able-bodied adults just quit working. Their financial freedom plummets, endangering the prospects of their spouses and children, too. It is devilishly difficult to reclaim a rewarding career after several years on the sidelines, especially with the breathtaking pace of technological change these days. Prosperity, once lost, does not always like to be found. From a societal perspective, economic dropouts no longer contribute to output, which affects everybody, rich and poor. It means weaker economic growth, fewer jobs, more people applying for government aid, lower living standards overall and greater pressure on those who have money to cough it up for the public good. That's the difference between 2015 and 1980.

Americans feel the strain, but not surprisingly, they aren't sure what's causing this economic malaise. It's like a low-grade illness you have a hard time explaining to your doctor but can't quite shake, either. Here are a few of the symptoms. Confidence in the legislative and judicial branches of the US government is near all-time lows, with confidence in the presidency nearly as bad. Such poor approval ratings are understandable given government shutdowns, pointless threats to default on the national debt and other destructive political stunts. Yet even if the government were choirboy earnest, it's not clear what new policies would fix problems that have a lot more to do with globalization and the digital revolution than with tax rates or federal spending levels. Americans didn't always think it was the government's job to solve economic problems, and in fact there's not much evidence federal policymakers have ever been able to wave a magic wand and conjure prosperity. The notion that a certain set of conservative, liberal or even centrist policies will fix what ails us is mostly a bunch of salesmanship ginned up by political consultants who know they're peddling bunk.

Here's how conflicted we are about the proper role of the government in the economy and in our lives: Two-thirds of Americans think the government is too large and unwieldy, a portion that has skyrocketed from less than one-third 15 years ago.[12] (Before that, polling organizations rarely even thought to ask the question.) But ask people which parts of the government ought to be cut, and they are flummoxed. When presented with 19 categories of spending that could be cut, a majority oppose cutting spending in 18 of them, including Medicare, Social Security, education, environmental protection and defense. The only exception is aid to needy people outside the United States, which accounts for an infinitesimal portion of federal spending, anyway.[13] Certain polls are carefully calibrated by the conservative and liberal interest groups conducting them to ask questions in a way designed to elicit desired responses—so there's irrefutable evidence that Americans want the size of the government slashed, or vastly expanded, or whatever the group's ideological goal may be. So people who want to be well-informed must be careful about where they get their information. But surveys by reputable nonpartisan groups such as Gallup, Harris and Pew Research consistently show that Americans are deeply ambivalent about government spending; they think it's too high in general, probably because they imagine much of it going to crony capitalists, sleazy politicians and somnambulant bureaucrats. But Americans like the programs that account for most spending, and when asked whether they'd be willing to cut them, most say no. American voters, it turns out, contradict themselves much like the politicians they elect to represent them. Imagine that.

The bottom line is that most Americans clearly feel they're getting a bad deal from Washington—when the facts show they're getting more back from the government than they're putting in, and more than prior generations got. So we're getting more while complaining more about what we get. At the same time, Americans increasingly feel like they're losing freedoms they used to have. In 2006, the percentage of Americans telling Gallup they felt satisfied with the freedom to choose what they want to do with their lives was 91 percent. It has since fallen to 79 percent—a startling decline in a relatively short period of time. The United States used to rank near the top on this index of freedom, alongside prosperous nations such as New Zealand, Australia and Sweden. It now ranks thirty-third on Gallup's freedom scale, sandwiched between Bahrain and Cameroon. Asking people about freedom while letting them define what the word means obviously leaves a lot of room for interpretation. If you lived in a dictatorship that underwent reforms and suddenly held bona fide elections, you might feel ecstatic about your newfound freedoms and vote your nation near the top. Or you might feel suddenly liberated if the discovery of some new mineral brought wealth to people who had never known it—even in a kleptocracy such as Russia. Still, the Gallup rankings do reveal that Americans mourn the loss of freedom on a scale usually associated with financial disaster or an outright threat to democracy. America, once the land of the free, seems to be morphing into the land of the formerly free.[14] That's because the Liberty Trap has snared millions, and may yet snare many millions more.

For more than a century, American schoolchildren have been reciting a 31-word pledge so easy to remember that most of us never even bother to consider what the words mean. A Baptist preacher named Francis Bellamy drafted the Pledge of Allegiance in 1892 as a way for youths to voice their patriotism.[15] Ever since, American kids have been reciting the pledge in robotic unison at schools across the country, usually learning the text before even possessing the brainpower to comprehend what "allegiance," "republic" and "indivisible" really mean. Like many other expressions of our freedom and heritage, the concluding words—"with liberty and justice for all"—have taken on the hollow ring of a tired, overused slogan. Is America a place where there is truly liberty for all? Most people would probably answer no. But liberty for all is an ideal we ought to strive for—improving ourselves and our society along the way— rather than a status report on American virtues. The United States was once widely animated by a quest for accomplishments beyond other nations' reach. Now, we're more likely to scoff cynically at the very notion of liberty for all, rather than apply earnest national effort to attain it.

This book extols liberty for all who are willing to earn it. It explains how the Liberty Trap disrupts freedom, while prescribing ways to stay out of the Liberty Trap and get out if you're stuck in it. This is a personal quest as well as a professional, journalistic one: I've wandered close to the Liberty Trap, putting my own financial freedom at risk. I hope never to do that again, but I can't completely control the consequences of choices I've already made. And as a midcareer professional approaching what are supposed to be my peak earning years, I face many other choices that will ultimately determine whether I end up looking back on my working life as successful or something else. Other people depend on me making smart choices, too, which raises the stakes even more. There are risks to action and risks to inaction. There are risks to being unprepared and risks to being so prepared I stick too closely to a careful plan and fail to adapt to changes I don't foresee. As I will explain later on, one of the biggest risks I perceive in my own half-lived life is overdependence on people and events I can't control, with an inadequate reservoir of self-reliance. There's a lot of that going around.

The proper role of government is a hot topic right now. But we, the people, ought to be the real topic of conversation, because our attitudes toward government and our choices about how we live are changing more than the government itself. We have grown accustomed to the idea that we're entitled to financial freedom, and somebody else—like maybe the Minister of Personal Entitlement—must have screwed up if that freedom is slipping away. It's the same with many other parts of our lives that have nothing to do with government: We've outsourced to others matters that are vital to our well-being, all too often putting our fate in the hands of strangers who have no stake at all in whether we succeed or flounder. This has happened like the proverbial boiling of a frog, in a gradual fashion that disguises the clear and present danger to the organism. Instead of creating, sustaining and fixing things ourselves, we rely upon others: technical experts, who know how to fix smartphones, automobiles and plumbing; medical experts to supply pills or treatments or just make us feel grateful for the attention; advice experts to help with relationships, financial problems and parenting. We rely on pundits to tell us who's right and wrong on arcane political matters that have taken on far more importance than they're worth. And we wait for economic rescue from unseen bureaucratic mandarins rather than formulating our own rescues.

The Liberty Trap began to form in the decades following World War II, during a vast expansion of economic and financial freedom. The years from 1945 to 1980 or so were perhaps the most remarkable period of wealth creation in the history of the world. Much of that wealth was created in America and stayed in America, giving rise to the supposedly mighty American middle class. Living standards rose rapidly during that time, creating the expectation that progress would always move forward at such a merry pace. A typical factory worker might have lived in a grimy tenement in the early part of the twentieth century, but in a three-bedroom suburban house by 1980. Working-class parents once had limited hopes for their kids, but college eventually became a common pathway to a better life for nearly any young American who wanted it, no matter how much money was in the family bank account. Americans came to believe every generation would automatically end up better off than the prior one, no assembly required.

It hasn't quite worked out that way. The pace of progress has slowed dramatically, and the group of Americans getting ahead has become a much more exclusive club. Innovation, which is what generates wealth, is still in high gear in places like Silicon Valley and a few other pockets of dynamism. But prosperity has become selective. Wealth is still being created, but it's flowing to a smaller subset of the population. Social mobility—the ability to rise above the circumstances you were born into—is going backward, with rich kids likely to remain rich but the odds increasingly stacked against those born without advantages. It's beginning to look as if the fantastically productive years following World War II were an anomaly, and as a nation we're going to have to settle for a less dynamic economy with fewer winners and more losers than we're used to.

Some of that is the ebb and flow of economic tides, but a lot of it is the Liberty Trap clamping down on unwitting suspects. That marvelous expansion of economic freedom after World War II made us complacent, and we began to undervalue certain freedoms because they came effortlessly. The truest and most lasting form of freedom is freedom you earn yourself, because you know the price and you know what it will take to replace it if it's lost. That's the kind of freedom earned through the crucible experiences of depression and war during the 1930s and 1940s, and through personal effort and self-determination for a few years afterward. Freedom given as a gift is a vulnerable kind of freedom because the recipient doesn't know the price and tends to assume there's more where that came from, no matter what the actual supply of freedom may be. In the decades following World War II, financial freedom became an embarrassment of riches, compared with the rest of the world, with fewer Americans having to earn it and more receiving it as a gift. Freedom became devalued.

Freedoms are like other vital resources: They're highly valued where they're scarce and taken for granted where they're abundant. Water is a precious commodity in arid regions yet barely noticed where it flows freely. Clean air is something you rarely think about until you travel somewhere so polluted breathing makes you choke. It's the same with liberty. We don't know how much we have until it begins to seep away unnoticed for a while and suddenly comes up short. And if you never learned how to obtain and safeguard liberty—because that postwar miracle made such efforts unnecessary—you're not likely to have the skills and instincts that will allow you to obtain it. Would anybody who has drunk from a faucet his entire life know how to dig a well? Highly unlikely. Worse, when you think all water comes from a faucet, and don't even know what a well is, you're going to end up parched and helpless if the faucet ever runs dry and nobody's around to fix it.

The biggest problem with today's economy is that there are no simple fixes—and we're not so good at nuanced public initiatives that can't be explained in a sound bite. Washington politicians will never tell you this, but you, dear citizen, are on your own. The government is overspent, and in the future it's going to do less for people and ask more of them, which it must do in order to reverse the excesses of the last 15 years. That's simple math. Even if federal finances were in better shape, extreme partisanship bent on mutual assured destruction seems likely to be the norm for a while, with no sudden outbreak of comity looming. The good news, however, is that prosperity and opportunity still beckon, as long as you stay out of the Liberty Trap or free yourself if you're in it. The winners will be those able to put into practice the resourcefulness and self-reliance Americans relish in theory. Pretending doesn't cut it anymore.

THREE

A SECRET USE FOR
BROKEN GLASS

AS THE GREAT RECESSION GAVE WAY TO AN ANEMIC recovery, many Americans wondered when the economy was going to get back to normal. Some of us, however, began to conclude it wasn't going to return to normal, because something had changed permanently. Part of my job as a journalist is to figure out the powerful forces reshaping the US economy. Some of those forces develop imperceptibly and build over time into something significant. Those are the changes hardest to grapple with. Others arrive with a punch, leaving no doubt about what has happened. Some events are punchier than others, and around this time, in the fall of 2012, Superstorm Sandy roared ashore in my part of the country, testing the self-reliance of millions and rendering many helpless. Anybody suspecting Americans had become too dependent on systems and strangers, while losing the instinct for self-preservation, suddenly had ample proof.

Sandy hit every state on the East Coast from Florida to Maine, with New Jersey and New York suffering the worst damage. Several towns along the Jersey shore were effectively wiped out, while lower Manhattan, other areas of New York City and parts of Long Island ended up swamped for days. Nearly 125 people died and tens of thousands were left homeless. Millions more learned to lower the bar in terms of the things they can safely take for granted. I was lucky. My home lost power for 10 days, but nothing got damaged, and I was able to spend most of that time with a friend who had power, Internet, cable TV and a house full of suburban refugees like me. Yet even those of us who were merely inconvenienced felt alarmed as the infrastructure everybody depended on basically collapsed. Literally overnight, we lost the freedom to move around, do many things we ordinarily took for granted and even help each other.

I realize I'm being what you might call a locaboor, whining about things that happen nearby and affect me while perhaps not getting nearly as worked up when similar things happen to other people far away. But these types of misfortunes are becoming a kind of shared misery among Americans who endure coastal storms, midwestern floods and tornadoes, western wildfires, the occasional California earthquake and even mass shootings. It's hard to tell if these things are becoming more frequent, though climate scientists do tell us global warming will probably produce more destructive weather events as time goes on. What is certain is that we're all gazing into each other's tragedies and woes with a more powerful lens than ever, thanks to the Internet and social media.

Have you ever endured a gasoline shortage? It's astonishing. Car owners, whether they realize it or not, consider their vehicles a fool-proof escape pod if they ever have to get out of Dodge. But if there's no electricity to power the gas stations, or people to run them, or trucks to supply them, and you can't fill up, you can only get as far as the gas in your tank will let you. And that's if the roads are open.

Superstorm Sandy was the first time in my adult life I've encountered a gasoline shortage, and, I hope, the last time. The suburbs, where I live, don't work without gasoline. It's like taking the books out of a library or the hormones out of a teenager: suddenly the thing just stops being what it is. The night before the storm, I scoffed at panicky drivers who were lining up to buy gas as if the apocalypse were coming. Three days later, I was out of gas and couldn't get any more. To escape the tristate disaster zone, I would have had to ride my bicycle at least 100 miles.

When I was a kid, power outages were an adventure. We'd light candles and dig out flashlights and hunker down in a sleeping bag by the fireplace. These days, power outages begin with sinister overtones. An interesting new wrinkle of life today is the very real threat of jihadis fueled by hatred of affluent Westerners trying to blow up bridges, tunnels, power plants, shopping centers, subway systems and as many infidels as they can. Where I live, in the long shadow of the 9-11 terrorist attacks, every unexplained outage triggers this immediate question: Is it happening again? Some of the most knowledgeable experts in the counterterrorism business are amazed it hasn't.[1]

There's another difference today. Consider how dependent you are on infrastructure you don't understand or have any control over. If you're like me, checking your email and your smartphone are among the first things you do in the morning, sometimes even before getting coffee or putting a robe on. Smartphones have become so indispensable that people have died trying to retrieve dropped or misplaced phones from dangerous places such as the frozen river beneath a bridge and a working trash compactor.[2] The Internet and the cellular network that give life to your phone are almost as essential to daily existence as air or water. This is new. We've enjoyed terrific advances in the speed and convenience of communication during the last two decades, but the cost of that has been a lot more vulnerability than most of us realize. Dependence is the antipode to liberty, and our growing dependence on complex systems we barely understand has drawn us ineluctably closer to the Liberty Trap, as if gently reeled in by a master fisherman.

If you want to test how dependent you are on the Internet or your cell phone, try living without it for a few days. There's a small off-the-grid movement that attempts to live like this all the time, though you never hear much about off-the-gridders because . . . they don't usually answer email or pick up the phone! There are also people who leave the grid briefly on vacations or self-finding pilgrimages, and typically return proclaiming themselves purified. Strangely, however, most such people don't stay purified. It's just too tempting to reconnect and plug back in.

Here's my own impression of the few days I've spent off the grid, here and there. First of all, it gets bloody boring since most of my news, music and other entertainment arrives via some kind of network these days. Those are the things that make me feel connected to the world. Sure, I can read books or play cards for a few hours, and if I'm outdoors it feels great to bike or hike or ski or just focus on the horizon instead of a computer monitor. But despite an intriguing "paleo" movement dedicated to the kind of primitive living our ancient ancestors were stuck with, most of us prefer modern conveniences to the point we're addicted to them. I'm addicted to them, and if there were a 12-step program for people like me, the waiting list would probably span a decade.

On top of that, we tend to maintain most of our important social contacts these days with the help of digital networking. Traditionalists think there's something superficial about this, but I don't. The myriad ways I can communicate with people—email, phone, text message, social networks and whatever will displace all of those things—has allowed me to connect with people more efficiently and be closer to the friends and family members I care about. Old fogies might be content to sit in the darkness using a fountain pen to write a letter by candlelight that the intended recipient won't read for a week, but as for me, if you take away my electronics, suddenly I get very lonely.

As things eventually got back to normal after Sandy, there was a lot of controversy over how the government should prepare better for such disasters, how the power companies should fortify key substations and how insurance companies should change their policies in coastal areas. But something was missing. There was hardly any discussion of how individuals should boost their own self-reliance in order to fare better when infrastructure fails. It was the same group-think that followed the Great Recession: Everyone looked outward for somebody to blame, somebody to fix the problem and somebody to bear the cost of making sure it didn't happen again. Hardly anybody changed their own behavior or willingly took responsibility for being better prepared next time. It didn't seem to occur to anybody that maybe their own self-reliance was suspect.

That bothered me. First of all, I felt ridiculously helpless during Sandy as I waited like everybody else for a gas station to open and a utility crew to fix whatever snapped wire had left my house in the dark. Was that the best I could do? At the time, I thought of myself as fairly resourceful. I knew how to change a flat tire, replace a light fixture, stitch a hole in clothing and perform other types of basic maintenance that amazed and delighted some of my friends, who had to call an expert for everything. I didn't worry about topping off my gas tank because I assumed I'd figure something out if gas actually ran out. What I ended up figuring out is I have a grandiose and exaggerated sense of my own resourcefulness. I knew practically nothing about how to survive on my own.

Sandy created so much lasting damage that it stayed in the news for months and generated all sorts of coverage of the different ways people reacted to the disaster. One day I read a *New York Times* article entitled "The Preppers Next Door," about people who prepare, to varying degrees, for a day when something terrible happens.[3] *Prepper* is an imprecise term that can include mild forms of disaster preparation, such as canning your own fruits and vegetables and keeping a few candles on hand. Gold bugs—people who stockpile gold in anticipation of an economic collapse in which currency and other types of paper assets become worthless—are preppers, in a sense. There's a whole disaster prep industry, including police, firefighters, paramedics, FEMA, the Red Cross and others who arguably are preppers by profession. But most people familiar with the term associate it with kooks who build underground bunkers, stockpile years' worth of supplies and do a lot of other things to prepare for end times, whatever they expect end times to be. Many such characters have found their way onto *Doomsday Preppers,* the National Geographic reality show that debuted in 2012.

I did some research and discovered that prepping is a booming business. There's a kind of trade group called the American Preppers Network (APN), whose Web site dispenses advice on sustainable living, survivalist gear, how to get started if you're interested in prepping and how to meet other preppers. I called them up and spoke with Mike Porenta, a spokesman for the APN who didn't sound kooky at all. He explained that modern prepping has evolved from a blend of traditional homesteaders who try to live off the land, former military guys comfortable living in the field, survivalist types distrustful of mainstream society and an eclectic mix of other folks who feel something worrisome is happening in America. Part of the movement emanates from Utah, where Mormons have a long history of stockpiling food and supplies in case adversity strikes. There have always been such people, but a few catalyzing events have brought them together and drawn many others to the cause. The first was the 2001 terrorist attacks in New York, Washington, DC, and Pennsylvania, which clearly showed the nation to be far more vulnerable to harm than most people thought at the time. Hurricane Katrina, in 2005, left thousands of people desperately stranded amid an appalling breakdown of leadership that showed how inept government can be when people need it most. The 2008 financial crisis was another institutional meltdown, with big banks that form the backbone of the entire economy suddenly so ruptured that the unthinkable—a full-blown depression—nearly happened. Every now and then, there's a pandemic—such as Ebola, or avian flu—that terrifies significant numbers of people, with movies such as *Contagion* fanning the fear. The Fukushima nuclear disaster in Japan in 2011 sent a radioactive plume toward America's West Coast and gave disaster aficionados one more danger to guard against.

Preppers aren't the type of people who voluntarily raise their hands so they can easily be counted, and the Census Bureau hasn't thought to keep track, either. So it's hard to know how many preppers of different stripes there are in the United States. But it does seem clear the movement is growing. Porenta told me the APN began in 2009 with a tiny Internet audience that has since grown to more than 120,000 unique visitors per month, a respectable following that's larger than a mere fringe group would attract. And APN's Facebook page has more than 120,000 likes. There are undoubtedly some hucksters trying to cash in on the popularity of prepping by peddling bogus advice, all sorts of survivalist gizmos people don't need and other such stuff—it wouldn't be capitalism without them. But some respectable businesses have grown up around the movement, too. A Utah company called Shelf Reliance has grown from a tiny start-up into a national firm that supplies canned food, shelving systems for high-volume storage and other types of survivalist supplies to huge retailers such as Sam's Club and Costco. *Inc.* magazine says Shelf Reliance's annual sales have grown more than 200 percent per year for the last several years.[4] I mentioned my interest in the prepping industry to a Wall Street analyst I know, and he gave me a one-word answer: Generac. This, it turns out, is a publicly owned company whose product line includes heavy-duty generators for business and residential customers. Sales have been growing by double digits, and Wall Street is keenly interested because for five years following the Great Recession, the stock price rose by nearly three times as much as the overall market. A lot of people were fortifying their homes against mayhem, and there was good money to be made.

I tracked down Arthur Bradley, who's the author of several prepper guidebooks, including the *Prepper's Instruction Manual* and *The Handbook to Practical Disaster Preparedness for the Family*. He also happens to be an electrical engineer at NASA, with a publicity photo that shows a smiling Bradley sitting at a desk, surrounded by computer equipment, wearing the government-issue Everyman outfit: a respectable plaid blazer and a white button-down shirt.[5] I figured he'd provide a rational perspective on the prepper phenomenon, and he did. "My message has never been to get off the grid or check out of modern society," he told me. "Instead, think about how to weather hurricanes or tornadoes. What if there's hyperinflation? Before you prepare for the end of world, prepare for things you know are more likely to happen." Bradley sounded like he, too, had been surprised by the level of interest in the topic, which explained why he kept writing books on prepping—a lot of people bought them. Still, he warned, "There are a great number of people in the nation with almost no preparation whatsoever. Our generation is spoiled. There's this trust that the government will just make things right. But if there's a big event, there's not enough money to make things right."

My research into prepping helped me realize there were other people, including some smart ones, asking the same questions I was asking about overdependence on the government and other institutions, a general lack of self-reliance and the types of things that could go wrong if events unfolded in a particularly unfortunate way. Preppers might be able to address a few practical concerns I had about myself and my own family: Should I have a generator in my house? Would a generator be enough? What about a store of gasoline to power the generator? (Some people who had generators during Sandy couldn't run them because they couldn't get gas. Yes. The irony.) What about stockpiling food? What about weapons to protect the things other people might want if they knew I had them? What about some means of escape other than a car? Is it legal, and practical, to float away from a disaster zone in a small hot-air balloon?

I had another reason for wanting to learn more about the preppers: to gauge whether they were better defended against the Liberty Trap than other people. Better than me, maybe. Were they more alert about safeguarding their freedoms and therefore less likely to give them up? Did greater self-reliance mean greater economic freedom? Or was it merely a nice skill set to develop just in case something terrible happens? On a broader level, were personal liberty and rugged individualism really thriving somewhere out there in America? If they were, I wanted to see for myself.

I got started by seeking out Jason Charles, the New York City firefighter who helped run something called the New York City Preppers Network. I first read about him in that *New York Times* article, and as I researched Charles a bit, it sounded like it might be an adventure just to meet him. He had been featured on one of the first episodes of *Doomsday Preppers*. The show typically features paranoid Americans preparing for some form of Armageddon, and sure enough, on the show Charles appeared in, he explained his concern about a supervolcano capable of blowing the lid off earth's atmosphere, clogging the air everywhere with ash.[6] The *New York Post* ran its own piece on Charles, calling him the "fringe fireman" and highlighting his habit of keeping a box of crushed glass near the front door of his apartment to scatter in the hallway during an emergency and keep marauders away.[7] Now that was something I never would have thought of on my own. I contacted Charles and he agreed to chat with me one Sunday afternoon at his apartment in Manhattan's Harlem neighborhood, a short drive from my own home in New York's leafy suburbs.

On a bleak winter day I drove to Charles's building, buzzed on the keypad next to the fortified steel door, took the elevator up a few flights and found my way to the apartment at the far end of the concrete hallway. While I was glancing around for broken glass, a burly guy in a muscle shirt and baseball cap, with tattoos running down both arms, swung open the door—as a grinning toddler clung to his legs. Charles invited me in and introduced me to his two young kids, as well as his black Labrador retriever, Tyler, all of whom seemed excited to have a visitor stopping by. His wife came out to say hi, then slipped away with the kids. Charles and I finally sat down in the kitchen as a pot of fragrant red sauce simmered on the stove. If a madman preparing for supervolcanoes and bandits lived here, he was a master of disguise.

Charles grew up in the 1980s in Washington Heights, which at the time was an urban battlefield police and fire crews routinely ignored. From his family's apartment windows, Charles could see Harlem to the south and the Bronx to the north. "Every night you looked out, you'd see fires burning," he told me. His family thought constantly about where to go if they had to flee a fire. As a kid, Charles started prepping for disaster by planning how to save his toys if his apartment building burned down.

He went to college in New York City and became an emergency medical technician, asking to be assigned to the busiest truck in Harlem (kids, don't try this trick at home). Then he became a firefighter in a similar neighborhood. Charles recounted a few stories about the depraved characters he had encountered on the job, which made it easy to understand how rabid looters banging on the door, to him, weren't just a theoretical concern. Still, he seemed to regret the loony prepper mystique that characterized his TV and newspaper cameos. "They dressed up a lot of things," he told me of the *Doomsday Preppers* episode. As a journalist, familiar with the ways of the media, I would have been faking it had I acted surprised.

Charles became an avid prepper after reading the bestselling 2009 novel *One Second After* by William Forstchen, which describes the mayhem that ensues after a nuclear bomb goes off in space, emitting a devastating electromagnetic pulse that fries every electrical circuit in America. That might sound nutty, but I had walked the halls of the Pentagon as a military correspondent earlier in my career, and I knew that the risk of an EMP was an old Cold War concern that still worried a few generals as nations such as North Korea and Iran developed nukes. Besides, Charles told me, his real concern wasn't an EMP or a supervolcano but a more plausible disaster such as a major hurricane that might turn Manhattan into a lake with some buildings sticking out of it. Given the chaos that Superstorm Sandy had caused, that didn't sound crazy at all.

In the chain of events Charles envisions, it's not some fantastical event that unleashes chaos. The terrifying turning point would come

when something goes wrong and then cops, firefighters, relief workers and other people who help keep public order start looking out for
their own families instead of showing up for work. That happened
to some extent in New Orleans when Katrina struck in 2005. "In
neighborhoods like this," Charles said, referring to his own turf in
Harlem, "when people notice there are no cops around because the
cops are protecting their own neighborhoods, then the low-income
neighborhoods will burn to the ground. When all this shit breaks
down, where do you think those people are going to go? To whoever
has money. If I have a job, that translates into I have money. All the
people with good jobs are gonna get knocks on their doors."

Hmmm. I had a good job, compared with people who harass
EMTs and firefighters for a living. Was I going to get a knock on
my door? A complete breakdown in social order wasn't something
I worried about very often, but then again, I never thought I'd be
stuck in a cold house for 10 days because I couldn't get gas to drive a
couple of hours to someplace more hospitable. Besides, Charles had
done way more research and planning than I had ever dreamed of. In
a hallway off the kitchen where we sat, there was a huge pile of gear
that turned out to be the contents of a "bug-out bag" built for four,
including survival equipment for Charles, his wife and their two kids
if they had to leave home and live off nothing more than they could
carry. There was even a bug-out bag for Tyler, the lab, who must
have been the best-prepared dog in New York. In the spare spaces
within his small apartment and in a nearby storage locker, Charles
had stowed enough food, water and other necessities to survive for
several months in case stores ran out of goods—or everything got
looted. He had a portable stove for cooking on the terrace and plenty

of military-style field rations if the smoke from the stove attracted unwanted attention and everybody had to eat inside. This was his "bug-in" plan, for laying low at home if that seemed like the best option in an emergency.

The bug-out plan was more complicated. Charles had made prior arrangements to stay with a variety of out-of-state friends and relatives if there was an emergency. The trick—as I could have told him!—was getting to them. Charles kept his pickup truck fully fueled, but he also knew that in a disaster, the roads may be impassible and the bridges that connect Manhattan to the rest of the world closed or even destroyed. So he had two inflatable rafts big enough to get him and his family across the Hudson River to New Jersey—and he knew precisely where the narrowest crossing point was. He was also thinking of buying a cheap used car and storing it on the New Jersey side of the river.

There was one key provision that couldn't be packed in a bag. "Being in shape is the most important part of the plan," Charles told me. To bug out according to his scheme, Charles figured he'd need to be able to walk 20 miles a day, with 100 pounds of gear on his back. Suddenly it dawned on me why genuine self-reliance was more popular in theory than in practice. "We've become a nation of fat people because we've lost the art of doing things for ourselves," Charles declared. Now that, I couldn't argue with at all.

As I got ready to leave, Charles may have felt we had strayed too far into the realm of the phantasmagorical. Despite his obsession with what could go wrong, he assured me, he and his family still lived normal lives. "We still go to the movies and take family vacations," he said. "It's just that I think of all the angles. When we go to Disney World, I ask myself, 'If we had to get out of here, how would we do it?'"

Was I thinking of all the angles? Did I even want to? The answers were "absolutely not," and "I'm not sure." I did some further research on disaster preparedness. It turns out mainstream organizations such as the Red Cross and the Centers for Disease Control and Prevention encourage everybody to be prepared to survive on their own for at least a few days if there's a major disaster, with no help from government or relief organizations. That struck me as funny, because I thought the whole point of the Red Cross was to show up after a disaster so you didn't have to float your family across a dangerous river on inflatable rafts. The Red Cross Web site includes detailed instructions on how to assemble a bug-out bag—which it calls a "preparedness kit"—including provisions for pets if you have them. New York City even started running cheeky TV commercials in which a family of four sits down at the dining room table and goes over a checklist for how to be unprepared and clueless if an emergency rises. "I'll pack the dead batteries," the son volunteers. "I'll only pack what I don't need into a duffel bag," the daughter says. "Perfect," the dad answers.[8] The city's Web site, meanwhile, has an entire section devoted to organizing a family "go bag" for use during an evacuation, and other tricks that could be right out of the prepper playbook. I lacked many items on the list. If that gives you the urge to snicker condescendingly, ask yourself this: Do you know where your iodine tablets are? Do you have an eyedropper handy for adding bleach to contaminated water? Have a Mylar blanket, or even know what one is?[9]

No, I wasn't thinking of all the angles. Not even close.

FOUR

GIVE ME INCANDESCENT LIGHT BULBS, OR GIVE ME DEATH!

WE HAVE SOME FUNNY WAYS OF THINKING ABOUT liberty in America these days.

We revere stories of the nation's founding fathers, who really did risk quite a lot for personal freedom and national sovereignty. During the American Revolution, George Washington accepted leadership of the ragtag Continental Army knowing the odds were long and the consequences would be severe if the British ever captured him. "In the event of defeat, Washington knew, he would be hanged as the chief culprit," Ron Chernow wrote in his biography *Washington: A Life*. Washington even planned ahead of time for how he would handle a death sentence handed down by the King of England: "He decided that he would 'neither ask for nor expect any favor from his most gracious Majesty.'"[1]

Other founders were just as courageous, inspiring generations of Americans to risk everything for their country and their comrades, a gallant tradition that continued through the Civil War; both World Wars; Cold War–era confrontations in Korea, Vietnam and many other places; and modern military engagements in the Middle East and Afghanistan. Many others besides those in uniform have made sacrifices that made America freer and better, including countless numbers of uncelebrated heroes who took a stand in some remote corner of the country where there were no TV cameras or appreciative onlookers. Then there are the martyred civilians made legendary by dying in the service of liberty, such as Abraham Lincoln, Martin Luther King Jr. and, in my own industry, news reporter Daniel Pearl.

American history basically overflows with larger-than-life tales of citizens devoted to the cause of liberty above all. Yet in recent years, the call of liberty has gotten a bit smaller. For instance, in the 113th Congress (the two-year session that began in January 2013), legislators introduced at least 20 bills invoking "liberty" as a cause and at least 149 bills invoking "freedom." These legislative marvels include: the Internet Poker Freedom Act, the Freedom to Fish Act, the Health Freedom for Seniors Act, the Reclaiming Individual Liberty Act, the American Liberty Restoration Act, the Freedom of Travel Act, the Letting Insurance Benefit Everyone Regardless of Their Youth (LIBERTY—get it?) Act, the Freedom Fuels Act, the Television Consumer Freedom Act and, of course, the Dairy Freedom Act.[2] If you're wondering what members of Congress do all day, aside from selling influence, now you know: They dream up phony ways to act patriotic. But don't be too impressed—most bills invoking liberty or freedom aren't really meant to pass, and never do. Their purpose is to show that the bill's sponsors care deeply about the freedoms of the fishermen, dairy farmers, insurers and Internet gamblers who fill their campaign coffers with donations.

Here are a few of the subrevolutionary causes that have drawn adherents during the last few years:

Endangered light bulbs. Remember the Light Bulb Freedom of Choice Act? If you do, but you're too ashamed to admit it, that's understandable. This bill, proposed in the House of Representatives in 2011, was designed "to provide for the repeal of the phase out of incandescent light bulbs unless the Comptroller General makes certain specific findings." This whole story is too tedious to bother relating in much detail, but in short, the government tried to speed the adoption of new lighting technology that would save a lot of money for everybody and help curtail air pollution once those oldfangled, globule-shaped incandescent bulbs that have been around for almost 100 years were phased out. The new bulbs are more expensive, but they use less energy and save money over the life of the bulb. Still, people who call themselves "patriots" rebelled, insisting the government had no right to dictate what kinds of light bulbs citizens must use. In a truly free country, the theory goes, people ought to be allowed to stick with retrograde bulbs decades after they became obsolete. The legislation generated a lot of press but didn't pass.[3]

Nineteenth-century medicine. The development of vaccines is "perhaps the greatest success story in public health," according to the Centers for Disease Control and Prevention.[4] Where vaccines are commonly administered, they've nearly eradicated diseases such as polio, smallpox, measles and meningitis. Without them, some of us wouldn't be alive or healthy today. But never mind all that. A lot of parents—egged on by celebrities such as Playboy model/actress/talk-show host/nondoctor Jenny McCarthy—have begun to view institutionalized medicine and government guidelines as bunk, and to make their own judgments about the value of vaccines. Result: a growing "anti-vax" movement, declining vaccination rates and the reemergence of nearly extinct killer bugs. Such parents are checking themselves into the Liberty Trap by inviting the ravages of serious illness into their families and threatening their own kids with a debilitating start to life.[5]

Unlimited weaponry. Here's an attempt at something novel: a rational chat about guns. Most Americans realize the Constitution, for better or worse, enshrines the right to bear arms. The highest rate of gun violence in the developed world has done virtually nothing to persuade the majority of Americans it might be worth considering a few changes to the nation's tradition of readily available firearms.[6] Yet there still exists the quaint and silly notion that it's important for ordinary folks to have the right to stockpile weapons just in case the government becomes tyrannical and the need arises to form local militias able to bushwhack the tyrants. Think about that for a minute. The US military is the most lethal and efficient fighting force in the history of the world (which is a good thing, by the way). And some twenty-first-century militia from Texas or Arizona, armed with assault rifles and maybe some surplus Soviet military gear, is going to give them a run for their money? Tell you what—I'll watch that drubbing from the bleachers. It's obviously important to keep the nation's leaders in check, but the only way to do that has always been through civilian control of the military and the ordinary rule of law. Guns might help defend against criminals, but could we please just drop the obsolete idea that some posse from Lubbock will save America from a rogue airborne brigade or a treasonous fleet of missile-firing drones? Honestly, the "well-regulated militia" clause of the Second Amendment is almost like a practical joke the founders played on their modern descendants.

The evil known as taxes. Paying taxes was once cool, believe it or not. During World War II, as Washington was hiking taxes on almost everybody to help pay for the war, songwriter Irving Berlin wrote a patriotic ditty called "I Paid My Income Tax Today," which Danny Kaye sang and hundreds of radio stations played.[7] Can anybody imagine popular celebrities encouraging Americans to pay their taxes today? If anything, public figures encourage us to do the opposite. Republican senator Lindsey Graham of South Carolina became a sort of folk hero a few years ago when he said on TV that "it's really American" to find legal ways to dodge taxes, even if it involves exotic overseas tax shelters most ordinary people can't access.[8] It's natural to consider taxes oppressive, yet we get a pretty good deal in the United States. Americans pay less in taxes, relative to the size of the economy, than citizens in any other industrialized nation.[9] Nobody likes paying taxes, but a well-functioning tax system is a hallmark of every thriving nation in the world. Successful societies are built around institutions that pool public resources in order to do things ordinary people can't do themselves, such as build roads, maintain public safety and provide standardized education. It may not be the best imaginable system, but it's better than the feudal anarchy you'd be left with if there were no taxes and everybody had to provide everything for themselves. Americans have legitimate gripes with the way their government performs sometimes, and the real frustration may not be that taxes are too high but that taxpayers don't get their money's worth. The government we get in return for our taxes feels like a bad deal. Still, it's myopic to vilify the Internal Revenue Service, which collects tax money but doesn't decide how it gets spent, and to characterize the payment of any taxes at all as a violation of personal freedom.

The oppressive Federal Reserve. America's central bank, formed in 1913, is an extraordinarily powerful but fairly benign bunch of bureaucrats compared with other government agencies. The Fed was designed to be resistant to political meddling (thank God), and its chair, unlike cabinet secretaries, is appointed by the president to a four-year term that can't be revoked if a new president takes office. The Fed undertook extraordinary and untested policies during the last several years to counteract a recession that would have become the first US depression since the 1930s if somebody hadn't started stacking sandbags. The Fed undoubtedly made some mistakes along the way, but it was also the only organization that acted aggressively to save the US economy and stayed on the case. (Congress tried but got distracted by a partisan bickerfest that still continues.) For all that, the Fed has become a convenient villain for liberals and conservatives alike, who complain that the Fed has thrown the little guy under the bus, emasculated the US dollar, opened the door to runaway inflation and somehow enslaved ordinary working people. "End the Fed," critics proclaim, eager to return to the pre-Fed days when financial panics were far more frequent and severe.[10]

The dreaded Obamacare. The Affordable Care Act, known as Obamacare, got off to a notoriously disastrous start in the fall of 2013 and is obviously a flawed solution to an immensely complex problem: finding a way to provide health-care coverage to the 40 million or so Americans who have none. But Obamacare has hardly turned into the job-killing, business-shutting, family-ruining, puppy-strangling, freedom-exterminating law that critics claim it is.[11] A core problem with Obamacare is that it harmed some people—by driving up their insurance costs or making their coverage invalid—in order to help others, which made it seem like an unfair and even sneaky transfer of wealth from one group to another. Still, the majority of Americans say the law hasn't affected them at all, which might mark the widest gap ever between public outrage over something done in Washington and the percentage of people that thing actually affects.[12] Some people, in fact, feel so bitter about Obamacare that they choose to forego insurance and pay a fine rather than accept health-care coverage simply because it's tainted by government involvement.[13] If that's exercising some type of freedom, it's the freedom to make impractical, self-destructive decisions out of pride, which neither the Declaration of Independence nor the US Constitution endorses.

Many of these anti-establishment tirades come from the so-called Tea Party, which coalesced early in the administration of President Barack Obama as an aversion to activist government and a nostalgic craving for simpler times that were never really all that simple. Related to that is a determined libertarian movement—represented by politicians such as retired representative Ron Paul and his son, Senator Rand Paul—that may be growing. Libertarians range in their views from moderate to severe, but in general they feel government should be as small as possible, individuals should be responsible for their own decisions—including bearing the full cost of bad decisions—and the free market should be left to itself. "Libertarians believe that as long as we do not violate others' rights, we should each be free to live as we choose," explains scholar Jason Brennan in *Libertarianism: What Everyone Needs to Know.* Various polls suggest libertarians could represent 15 to 25 percent of American voters, with some people probably drifting in and out of this belief set based on how well or poorly they feel government is working.[14]

The media tends to create the impression that the modern quest for liberty in American is the ranting of a small coterie of cranks. That's far too glib. Disillusionment has become a chronic national condition that afflicts all sorts of people, regardless of political party or even income. Trust in government and other big institutions Americans have long relied upon—banks, big companies, churches,

HMOs, public schools, the press—is near historic lows among liberals and conservatives both.[15] Maybe that's no surprise given dithering politicians, financial meltdowns, overpaid CEOs, rapacious priests, overpriced medical care, students who can barely read and the scandal-obsessed shallowness in my own industry, the media. Still, it all adds up to a momentous and disturbing cultural shift. "In Nothing We Trust," the *National Journal* declared in a story exploring the sweep of cynicism across the country: "Americans are losing faith in the institutions that made this country great."[16]

There are two basic reasons for this. The first is that the economy has been moving in reverse for too many people. The growing wealth gap between the rich and the rest wouldn't be that big a deal if prosperity were widespread and it felt like everybody was getting ahead—the way it did, more or less, in the 1980s and 1990s. But what's happening instead is the wealthy are making huge gains while average people are drifting backward. Median household income, adjusted for inflation, peaked in 1999, then drifted down in a jagged pattern for more than a decade.[17] At the current weak pace of growth, there could be a 20-year divot before median incomes surpass the prior peak. Yet bankers and CEOs and tech titans are richer than ever. Something's obviously wrong—and the institutions that once helped generate prosperity seem to have something to do with it.

The second problem is politics—but maybe not the way you imagine. Sure, Washington is a mess. Republicans and Democrats hate each other, compromise is dead, blah blah blah. But there have been many eras of nasty partisan politics arguably worse than what we've had lately: the huge antiwar demonstrations during the Johnson and Nixon administrations; McCarthyism and the "Red Scare" during the 1950s; FDR's cunning vilification of the wealthy during the Depression; and on and on, back to the populist Jacksonian revolution of the 1830s and the violent founding of the country itself. What's genuinely new about politics is the Internet. Never before have there been so many people voicing so many opinions about politics to such a large audience, often with no accountability for truthfulness. Washington, DC, covers a scant 61 square miles, the equivalent of a microbe on the US landmass. Yet the Washington press corps is now roughly twice the size it was during the Watergate scandal in the 1970s, when the mainstream press actually had a good reputation.[18] There are fewer newspapers and magazines represented in Washington than there used to be, but a lot more small niche organizations, most of them Web sites and some of them far more concerned with a political agenda than with dispassionate facts. Social media services such as Twitter and Facebook make it even easier for anybody to express an opinion that echoes among millions and stokes controversy, if that's the desired outcome. Outside the capital, meanwhile, traditional news organizations have closed bureaus that used to bring us news from Philadelphia, Atlanta, Dallas, Denver, Seattle and many other places where actual people still live. Nobody calculates the numbers, but I'd wager that at least half the nation's journalistic muscle covers Washington, which accounts for just two-tenths of 1 percent of the nation's population and 3 percent of its GDP.[19] Whatever the number, the media presence in Washington is way too large, with many news and quasi-news organizations duplicating each other's efforts and magnifying the impact of small events or even nonevents that would barely affect most people if not broadcast worldwide. The rest of the country (celebrities excepted) receives far too little attention. Today's media specializes in a kind of vapor news that isn't necessarily about anything that happens but about what Newsmaker 1 says, what Newsmaker 2 says in response, and what Newsmakers 3 through 100 think the verbal sparring really means.

This is a problem because it has overpoliticized the entire country, creating the impression that our political freedom is endangered. People form strong opinions about arcane political matters such as the usefulness of the Senate filibuster or the intricacies of foreign policy or the legitimacy of the Export-Import Bank of the United States. All too often, people form die-hard opinions on things they know little about because a favored commentator on the left or the right basically told them what they should think. I'm not saying ordinary people aren't smart enough to form intelligent opinions about public affairs. Mostly, they are. But I am saying that having informed opinions requires effort and self-education and the patience to gnaw through tedious subject matter that bores most people, including me a lot of the time. It's easy to pretend complex issues are as simple as black or white, yes or no, for or against; discarding nuance absolves you from having to learn more and perhaps uttering the great lost phrase "I don't know." Yet we seem to live in a time when everybody knows already, because there is always somebody, somewhere, who seems authoritative enough, telling you what you want to hear and convincing you it's safe to believe it. When you take a stand on something simply because somebody else says you should—without truly evaluating the pros and cons yourself—you have surrendered intellectual freedom, with a loss of financial and economic freedom likely to follow.

People believe what they want to believe because many of these political issues are proxy battles. The core issue, which you'll strike if you probe deeply enough, is that too many people feel threatened—by cultural changes they don't understand, by technology that seems to propel everybody forward except them, and most of all by a turbulent economy that's leaving millions financially stranded. Part frustration and part fear, this impulse takes the form of political warfare because the vapor news overflows with oversimplified morality tales full of faux heroes and faux villains. With a lot of people feeling defeated and looking for somebody to blame, and the media always ready with a full lineup of bogeymen to choose from, we have become a nation of blamers who see each other in the extremes necessary to depersonalize and vilify.

The people running Washington, DC, know all this and relentlessly exploit the vapor media and the ordinary people who consume it for their own benefit. When Newt Gingrich was a rising firebrand politician from Georgia, he told a group of fellow conservatives, "The number one fact about the news media is they love fights. You have to give them confrontations. When you give them confrontations, you get attention; when you get attention, you can educate."[20] *Educate* doesn't really seem to be the word for it these days, but *mislead* might do, or *manipulate,* or *distort* or certainly *pander.* Other than that, Gingrich, regrettably, was right. The cynicism in Washington is so profound that one of Gingrich's most lasting legacies was the strategy of destroying the institution in order to save it: bringing Congress to such a dysfunctional standstill that disgust with the government grew like a tumor, leading to the only rational course of action—shrinking the tumor through radical surgery.[21] This has actually become a standard political strategy. It wouldn't happen, of course, if the vapor media weren't a willing participant in the charade, reporting every political maneuver as if it were something really important, like trash talk during the week leading up to the Super Bowl. Whenever there's the threat of a government shutdown or fiscal calamity or some other man-made fiasco in Washington, political nihilists are in the background like venal puppet masters, working the strings for enablers in the vapor media content not to peer too deeply into the shadows. With mutual assured destruction now the norm in national politics, this fear-mongering creates the impression that everybody's rights are threatened, as if we're locked in a cycle of tribal retribution. Conservatives aim to reverse the liberal agenda of the last administration, which corrected the abuses of the prior conservative administration, which happened because the liberals went overboard, which was a reaction to conservatives run amok, ad nauseam. It's actually in each party's interest to convince its adherents their political freedom is threatened, because that brings in donations needed to keep the Huns (aka, the other party) from gaining even more power and abolishing our very way of life.

I have a recurring fantasy in which the media stops reporting on anything that happens in Washington, forcing Americans to evaluate their sense of well-being based on changes that actually occur in their lives rather than dire warnings about what might happen if some wayward policy gets adopted in Washington or other types of political fear-mongering eagerly fanned by the media. (There's also a competing fantasy: the media stops reporting on celebrities, forcing us to stop gawking at other people's lives and do something more interesting with our own.) With nobody in town to broadcast their messaging, there would be no dueling press conferences in which Republicans and Democrats muster their cynical talking points in a never-ending battle of sophistry. Governing would be about doing, not talking. A lot of political strategists would lose their jobs. If there was nothing that needed to be done, the politicians would go home instead of holding inflammatory hearings meant to foment outrage. Come election time, voters would cast their ballots for candidates with a record of accomplishment and reject those without one. The press would have to report real stories about real people in the real world instead of hyping the backroom drama of politicking and inventing rise-and-fall narratives about people in suits going to meetings.

Okay, back to reality. My fantasy isn't going to come true, of course, no matter how many of my fellow journalists might agree with me (and many do). But something else important is going on. Americans are finally beginning to reject the false choice between a bad political party (whichever one you belong to) and a worse political party (the other one). They are reclaiming political freedom. People who describe themselves as being politically independent now account for nearly half of all adult Americans, the highest level in Gallup's history of tracking.[22] That's obviously more than those who consider themselves either Democrats or Republicans. That doesn't mean a viable third or fourth party is likely to develop, as some voters would like, because the corrupting influence of campaign donations heavily favors incumbents and the status quo, and makes it nearly impossible for a party with no Congressional committee assignments to raise money or gain traction. That may make voters even more disgusted, however, and they're registering their disdain by thumbing their noses at both parties and committing to neither. Even without a third party to represent them, independents—typically pragmatic and centrist rather than ideological or venal—have become the must-win voting bloc national candidates can't ignore.

To sum up all this venting in one depressing diagnosis, the overall problem with American politics involves "profound changes in mass media, the coarsening of American culture, the populist distrust of nearly all leaders except those in the military, and the insidious and destructive role of money in politics and in policymaking," according to Thomas Mann and Norman Ornstein in their forceful book *It's Even Worse Than It Looks.*[23] These factors began to converge in the 1990s, when the economy was booming, unemployment wasn't a problem and the United States could afford to have lousy government. Things are a lot tougher now, with a much higher bar for success, more competition throughout the world and less margin for error. We need strong national leadership at precisely the moment there isn't any. It's easy for people with strong political views to blame it on the opposition party, but in reality the US political system gives considerable power to the minority party, requiring compromise and unity to work effectively. With a legislature composed largely of millionaires—from both parties—who enjoy an ever-expanding set of perks most of their constituents can barely imagine, it really is everybody's fault in Washington.

Is there much any ordinary person can do about this? Not really. Are you powerless? Absolutely not. You can be a freedom forfeiter, if you choose, by forming an identity around issues created by politicians who live in a different world—figuratively and geographically—and devoting your physical and emotional energy to whatever those people decide is important. But if your sense of purpose and belonging comes from this type of partisan affiliation, you inhabit the Liberty Trap because you have surrendered an identity of your own and forfeited political freedom. If, on the other hand, you get your sense of purpose and belonging from other sources—like maybe your family, your community, your work, a creative pursuit or some cause you feel emotionally devoted to—you have a lot more personal freedom and you will make more decisions for yourself. You'll devote most of your mental energy not to political issues or public affairs, but to matters of home, hearth, heart and soul. I'm willing to bet light bulbs won't make the list.[24]

FIVE

THE FIVE ENDANGERED FREEDOMS

ASK YOURSELF A SIMPLE-SOUNDING QUESTION: WHAT is liberty?

You'll quickly discover it's not a simple question at all.

There are many popular conceptions of liberty. There's the teenager version: it's the freedom to do whatever I want. The Tea Party version: it's the freedom to live my life without the government in my face. Feminists: the freedom to make my own decisions about my body. Frightened seniors: the freedom to get back from the system what I put in. The underprivileged: the freedom to have a fighting chance. Redistributionists: the freedom for everybody to have a fair share. The wealthy: the freedom to keep what is mine. The indignant: the freedom to take back what has been taken from me. Militants: the freedom to take whatever I want. Pacifists: the freedom to forgive you for being militant. Religious fundamentalists: the freedom to oppose moral decay. Hollywood celebrities: the freedom to be the most important person in the world. Civil libertarians: the freedom to curse the country where I live. Politicians: the freedom to overuse the word *freedom*. Journalists like me: the freedom to exercise the First Amendment, and get paid for doing it.

Which definition of liberty do you subscribe to? And have you always believed that? Or have you changed your mind over time?

I'll speak for myself. There are times when I've felt pacifistic and times when I've felt militant. When I was younger, I was something of a redistributionist. As I get older (and my tax rates go up), I'm becoming more defiant about holding on to what I feel is rightfully mine. There are times when I feel I'm not getting my fair share and other times when I want the government to get its greedy hands out of my pockets. And I'm pretty sure than when I "retire," whatever that will mean in 20 or 30 or 40 years, I will feel that my freedom to get back out of the system what I put in will be threatened.

The point is obvious: Liberty and freedom mean different things to different people at different times in their lives, and those viewpoints can conflict—sometimes in turbulent and even violent real-world confrontations. One person's liberty is another's oppression, even in America, the land of the free. So anybody who genuinely cares about liberty needs to understand what it really means, beyond one's own parochial interests and the boundaries of a ZIP code.

In early 1940, Franklin D. Roosevelt, newly elected to a third presidential term, gave his famous "four freedoms" speech. The United States would soon be drawn dramatically into World War II after the Japanese bombed Pearl Harbor. And pressure was mounting for the United States to buck its isolationist bent and join the fight in Europe against Nazi Germany, which was overrunning much of the European mainland and bombarding Great Britain. FDR prepared extensively for the speech and revised it several times with the aid of his closest advisers. The "four essential human freedoms" didn't appear until the fourth draft, after FDR had stared silently at the ceiling for an unusually long time, then leaned forward in his chair and methodically dictated them to an aide.[1]

FDR's four freedoms are the freedom of speech, the freedom of every person to worship God in his own way, the freedom from want and the freedom from fear. More famous than FDR's speech may be Norman Rockwell's paintings depicting the four freedoms, which in the usual Rockwell fashion captured the wholesomeness and ambition Americans like to attribute to themselves. Rockwell initially offered the paintings to the War Department, but bureaucratic ineptitude being nothing new, the department never responded. So Rockwell offered them instead to the *Saturday Evening Post,* which published them in 1943. With the United States now deeply involved in the war, thousands of readers requested full-color prints.[2]

Whether deliberately or not, Roosevelt highlighted two distinctly different types of freedom: positive freedom and negative freedom, as British philosopher Isaiah Berlin and others have described them. Positive freedom is having the capacity to do something, such as expressing yourself, worshipping or, for that matter, skateboarding in the park or jumping out of an airplane. It's not the obligation to do it, just the ability to do it if you choose to. Negative freedom is the freedom from constraints, impediments or interference, which is what Roosevelt was getting at with his freedom from fear and freedom from want. Positive freedom is the freedom *to do* something. Negative freedom is freedom *from* some type of oppression. Or as Jason Brennan puts it in *Libertarianism,* "negative liberty is the absence of obstacles; positive liberty is the presence of powers or abilities."[3] Scholars generally think that negative freedoms are fundamental liberties that make positive freedoms possible. You must first have freedom from want, a negative liberty, before you can take advantage of your ability to get rich from your abilities as an engineer, basketball player or bikini model, which is a positive liberty. The distinction becomes important when pondering which freedoms we have and which we lack.[4]

Americans tend to think there was no such thing as freedom before 1776, as if the United States patented the cause and licensed it to others around the world. Not exactly. Perhaps the first known reference to freedom comes from stone tablets created in the Sumerian region of Mesopotamia around 2350 BC, which contain a word, transliterated as *amagi,* that means freedom or something like it. In literal terms, the word means "return to the mother," and scholars think it may refer to people being set free after being enslaved for debt.[5] Nearly 2,000 years later, Pericles, the leader of Athens during the Peloponnesian War, spoke of freedom and democracy in his famous funeral oration of 430 BC. "The freedom which we enjoy in our government extends also to our ordinary life," he declared. "There, far from exercising a jealous surveillance over each other, we do not feel called upon to be angry with our neighbor for doing what he likes, or even to indulge in those injurious looks which cannot fail to be offensive."[6] Today, "injurious looks" are better known as the death stare, which apparently had no place in ancient Athens.

From the very beginning, freedom has been driven by commerce and economic needs, rather than the other way around. "Homo sapiens became the wisest of primates around 40,000 years ago, when we learned to make deals with strangers," write scholars David Schmidtz and Jason Brennan in *A Brief History of Liberty*. "Neanderthals disappeared and modern humans flourished because the former were not entrepreneurs." Trade generated innovation, such as the division of labor, in which individuals specialize in one thing and team up with others who specialize in other things, which is a far more efficient way to produce stuff than every single person making his own sandals and growing his own food from scratch. Another breakthrough innovation was currency, which helped traders advance past the barter system and aided the division of labor. Coinage—small denominations of currency—was a particular contributor to economic liberty because it allowed the little guy to participate in trade much more vigorously than was possible under the barter system.[7] Even in ancient times, such innovations helped create wealth and push living standards upward, just as modern innovations such as indoor plumbing, air conditioning and automobiles have. The generation of wealth created an incentive to develop property rights and the rule of law, which are hallmarks of civilization and correspond closely with societies that have become prosperous (and vice versa). Prosperity isn't the same thing as liberty, but people in prosperous societies usually have far more freedom than people living in privation.

Since trade can cause harm—just like fire and water and other elemental necessities—it has also been an age-old contributor to bondage as well as a wellspring of prosperity. From almost the beginning, trade inevitably led to credit, with some borrowers unable to pay what they owed. It was common in ancient times for people who defaulted on their debts to be yoked into slavery, which, as gruesome as it must have been, had a side benefit: "The advent of slavery . . . sharpened the awareness of the difference between being and not being free," Schmidtz and Brennan write.[8] Outright slavery, of course, has been abolished in the developed world, but the brutal treatment of debtors persisted well into the 1800s, in the form of Dickensian debtors' prisons and other torments. The development of a forgiving bankruptcy code, in fact, was another breakthrough that fostered entrepreneurship and gave economic liberty a quantum boost. The United States was among the first nations to give honest people who defaulted on their debts a second chance, a practice virtually all democratic nations have enshrined.[9]

What's relatively new is our modern focus on individualism and especially the idea that the individual ought to be the focal point of all freedom, rather than some form of community or society. Ancient Athens was one of the few societies of its time in which there was a premium on personal freedom. In rival Sparta, freedom meant not living under the rule of another city-state, and in true martial form, the ruling culture was one in which individuals were subordinate to the good of the community. For the next 2,000 years or so, deep thinkers including Jesus Christ, Genghis Khan, Thomas Hobbes, David Hume, Adam Smith and America's founding fathers probed and debated the many ins and outs of liberty. Be assured, the basic question—What is liberty?—still has not been settled conclusively.

In America today, there's a sizable perception gap between the freedoms we actually have and the freedoms we think we have. For one thing, "the land of the free" isn't quite as free as its citizens may believe. We probably earn the prize for jabbering the most about liberty, but in an annual report on economic freedom published by the Fraser Institute, a Canadian research organization, the United States ranks seventeenth out of 152 countries. New Zealand, Switzerland, Canada and Australia all rank higher, which may not sound surprising, but so do the United Arab Emirates, Bahrain, Chile, Jordan and Estonia.[10] Methodologies can tilt such rankings in favor of smallish, fairly homogenous places with high per capita quantities of valuable natural resources. But other surveys corroborate the upsetting possibility that America isn't as free as its slogans suggest. In its own index of economic freedom, the Heritage Foundation, a conservative think tank, ranks America tenth, behind many of the same countries that score highly in the Fraser rankings.[11] The World Economic Forum ranks the United States a respectable fifth in its annual ranking of global competitiveness, but on subindicators that reflect various types of freedom, the United States scores much lower. It ranks forty-first out of 148 countries on the quality of primary education, forty-seventh on the ease of starting a business, fiftieth on public trust in politicians and ninety-fifth on the rate of mobile phone subscriptions.[12] And while some countries are rising in such rankings, the United States is generally drifting lower. As recently as 2008, for instance, the United States ranked first in the World Economic Forum's overall competitiveness ranking.

Many of our freedoms expand or contract with the state of the economy, since prosperity breeds freedom and vice versa. Yet the price of freedom in America generally remains so low that we don't appreciate how precious it is. Most of us know the old saying "freedom isn't free," which is etched on the Korean War Memorial in Washington,

DC, and is meant to acknowledge the sacrifices made by members of the military and others to attain or protect freedom. But for most people lucky enough to live in America, freedom actually is free. And that may be a big problem, because we tend to undervalue things that are free, even when they might be precious and quite costly to somebody else. It's extraordinary, really. Hardly anybody serves in the US military anymore, or is asked to serve their country in any way, which is why the tiny portion of Americans who actually volunteer for military service justifiably call themselves "the other one percent." One of the most decadent freedoms, in fact, may be enjoying freedoms that have been out of reach of most people throughout the entire history of the world, after having done nothing at all to earn them. "Our liberty today is, in so many ways, unprecedented," Schmidtz and Brennan write. "The future has never seemed so undetermined and unconstrained."[13]

It sure doesn't feel that way, though, does it? About 15 percent of the US population—roughly 47 million Americans—live in poverty.[14] With poverty comes bondage. "Poverty is a great enemy to human happiness," British sage Samuel Johnson wrote. "It certainly destroys liberty, and it makes some virtues impracticable, and others extremely difficult."[15] A lot of people well above the poverty line don't feel terribly free, either. Nearly half the US population consider themselves to be struggling or suffering, according to Gallup.[16] Even the wealthy tend to suffer from "affluenza" and a compulsion to keep up with others who will always be one step ahead. For the most part, Americans ought to be exalting in the orgy of freedom we enjoy. Instead, we are edgy, dour and insecure. "The translation of rising wealth into rising happiness is not automatic at an individual level," Schmidtz and Brennan write. "There are many ways in which people are adept at snatching defeat from the jaws of victory."[17]

Here's an example of how we have overpoliticized the concept of freedom and muddled its meaning. A group called the Mercatus Center at George Mason University publishes a ranking of "freedom in the 50 states" that lists New York state dead last in overall freedom, forty-eighth out of 50 in personal freedom, fiftieth in economic freedom, forty-seventh in property rights and fiftieth in "family friendliness." You might think the only people who would live in such a place are convicts assigned to a penal colony. Well, I live in New York state, in the suburbs just beyond New York City. I chose to live there and even to buy a house there, fully aware that it can be a challenging place to live. I have no regrets. Sure, the cost of living can be painfully high, and I'd probably have a bigger garage and maybe even a swimming pool if I lived in Akron or Omaha. Yet the area around New York City has a remarkably dynamic economy and rich cultural offerings that make it a terrific place to live—and raise kids, whether it's family-friendly or not. North and South Dakota have the highest freedom rankings in the Mercatus survey, and I could move there if I wanted to. No offense to Dakotans, but I don't want to. And if you read the details of how the Mercatus Center determines its rankings, you'll see they're based largely on things such as each state's fiscal and regulatory policies, laws regarding labor unions and workers' compensation (less of each equates with more freedom), gun-control laws, smokers-rights protections, helmet laws for motorcyclists, alcohol taxes and even the right to smoke pot and drive with open containers of booze in your car. If you're a true libertarian, maybe you care deeply about such policies whether they affect you directly or not. But if you're a union member, a parent of a kid with a motorcycle or somebody who feels threatened by the presence of firearms, you might have some major disagreements with the way Mercatus characterizes freedom. "We happily concede that different people value aspects of freedom differently," the authors of the rankings acknowledge on the Mercatus Web site.[18] True enough. I've lived in several states, and I don't think I've ever woken up feeling repressed because of a marijuana policy or helmet law.

To figure out why so many people in one of the freest places on earth seem to feel their freedoms are threatened—and are even unwittingly surrendering their freedoms through their own fear or inaction—I categorized the different types of freedom that seem relevant today. Here's my list of the 11 freedoms that matter:

Religious freedom: the ability to worship as you wish.

Political freedom: the ability to participate in government and have your views represented by officials you help elect.

Financial and economic freedom: exposure to opportunity and the ability to get ahead if you apply yourself. (One could argue that financial and economic freedom are two different things, in that the first involves an individual's money and wealth while the second entails a broader set of societal standards. Yet they're closely related, and both contribute to personal liberty.)

Freedom from conflict: living without fear for your safety.

Legal protections: confidence in the legal system to protect your rights, including civil liberties.

Self-reliance: the ability to take care of yourself with minimal dependence on others, especially if something goes wrong and normal resources aren't available.

Good health: no debilitating conditions that impair your other freedoms or impose unusual personal costs.

Temporal freedom: a reasonable amount of choice in how you spend your time.

The freedom to make mistakes: you can screw up and get a second chance without being inordinately punished.

Intellectual freedom: the ability to understand the world you live in and educate yourself about it.

Psychological freedom: good mental health and the ability to feel happy.

This is an imperfect list, as any list is. There's no "correct" list of freedoms, just as there is no correct flavor of ice cream. Your views will depend on your life experience and many other variable factors. But creating a taxonomy of freedoms allows us to take the next step, which is to figure out which freedoms we ought to worry about and which we can feel relatively secure about. By my estimation, five of the freedoms on the list are threatened, while the others are secure or even improving. Here are the five endangered freedoms, with a brief explanation of why we ought to worry about them:

Financial freedom: Prosperity is becoming harder to achieve and maintain.

Self-reliance: We're becoming overdependent on institutions and infrastructure at a time when they are becoming less reliable.

Temporal freedom: Multitasking, continual connectivity and a rising bar for success leave us less time to reflect, relax and enjoy what we have.

The freedom to make mistakes: A Darwinian economy leaves less margin for error.

Intellectual freedom: A flood of information, mostly flowing over the Internet, has made it harder, not easier, to figure out what's really going on.

Political freedom is not on my endangered list. There's certainly an ebb and flow to political freedom, and if wealthy political donors continue to capture an outsized amount of influence, political freedom might be on a future iteration of the list. But from a historical perspective, the rights that come with our form of self-government are getting stronger, especially civil rights. The real risk to political freedom is intellectual servitude, the knowledge gap between political operatives bent on manipulating the electorate and voters who don't even know they suffer from an information disadvantage—often, a huge one. The Wizard of Oz seemed terrifying when he was able to convince his subjects he was an angry and powerful sorcerer, but harmless and ridiculous when he lost his information advantage and was outed as a bumbling mortal. Politicians rely on a similar type of intellectual intimidation. They build power by persuading constituents of the terrible things that will happen if a challenger or opponent wins the seat. Voters contribute to the politicians' power—and forfeit their own political freedom—when they're so bamboozled they believe it. So political freedom is on my endangered list, in a way, with intellectual freedom as its proxy.

Many people will quibble with my list of endangered freedoms, or argue that other freedoms are more endangered than the five I have listed. There are undoubtedly some Muslims, Jews and probably even Christians who feel religious tolerance has gotten worse, not better, especially since the 2001 terrorist attacks in New York and Washington and the subsequent wars in Afghanistan and Iraq. There are still gays who feel maligned and discriminated against. And I have no doubt that every kind of racism ever invented still persists in some virulent, cellular form, interfering with many people's freedom.

But consider, for a moment, the progress we've made in enhancing some very important freedoms. Mass shootings, child abductions and other sensational crimes may create the impression we live in a lawless society—especially given saturation coverage on cable news and Internet sites. But the violent crime rate has actually dropped by nearly 50 percent during the last 20 years, according to FBI data.[19] That's a sharp improvement in freedom from conflict. More than 50 percent of Americans now say they support same-sex marriage according to Gallup, which is double the level of support in the mid-1990s.[20] The Pentagon now allows gays in the military, a once-unthinkable change that reflects expanding freedoms for many (but not, admittedly, for traditionalists who feel threatened by gays). It is almost considered unremarkable at this point that America elected a black president for not one but two terms, proving it wasn't a fluke. Whether you like Barack Obama or not, the fact that Americans could elect him shows that the march of freedom, as it were, continues.

So let's pay attention to the freedoms that are deteriorating—and try to figure out *why* they're endangered so we can do something about it. Are these freedoms threatened because of outside forces? Or because individuals compromise their own freedom? Or both? For the five endangered freedoms, the answer is both. Sure, there may be bad policies coming out of Washington or unfair competition from China or some other external factor impinging on freedom. But quite often, there are things ordinary people can do to counteract such threats. And too many people are not doing that. Freedom suffers the most when people are passive in the face of danger, which is happening now. The Liberty Trap is a trap because we don't have to let ourselves get snared in it. But we do.

Financial and economic liberty is the freedom most threatened in American today. It is, in fact, getting harder to get ahead. The middle class is severely strained and probably shrinking. It's less and less likely that people born without wealth will attain it. And even though we shun British-style titles and inherited privileges, an unofficial aristocracy has formed in America, and it's muscling in on the meritocracy we like to think allows anybody to join the upper class. Assuming this trend will correct itself could be an awful mistake. "Things are going to get much worse for the United States and other advanced economies in the years ahead," says Stephen D. King, chief economist of the big British bank HSBC. "We are reaching end times for Western affluence."[21] He's not a lone worrier. In the surprise best seller *Capital in the Twenty-first Century*, French economist Thomas

Piketty warned we are in the early phase of a new Gilded Age in which the rich will become even more empowered while everybody else will fight for a dwindling share of the pie.[22] These gloomy diagnoses might turn out to be wrong, but the stresses behind them—economic disruption, a growing gap between the rich and the rest, fraying social-safety nets and lousy government policies—are very real and will take a toll one way or the other.

Choking off financial freedom generates volatility and sometimes even revolution. It helped give rise to Hitler, Stalin and many other tyrants. A lack of economic opportunity is a key reason too many young Islamic men become jihadi militants instead of university students or entrepreneurs. When financial freedom is threatened, people look for somebody to blame for their declining fortunes. Tensions rise. The economy shifts from a positive-sum society in which everybody can get better off at the same time to a zero-sum society in which somebody must lose wealth in order for somebody else to gain it.[23] America obviously isn't a dictatorship, but it's not on the top of its game, either. Two political science professors, Martin Gilens of Princeton and Benjamin I. Page of Northwestern, argued in a recent groundbreaking study that "America's claims to being a democratic society are seriously threatened" because "economic elites" wield all the political power. "The preferences of the average American appear to have only a minuscule, near-zero, statistically non-significant impact upon public policy," they concluded.[24] You don't need to flee to Canada just yet, but every American ought to be aware of the tectonic changes that are transforming our economy and society. Even if the worst-case scenario doesn't occur, it's highly likely the US economy will grow more slowly during the next decade or two than it has during prior decades. That alone will depress living standards for millions of Americans. This is why America is undergoing a kind of societal fracturing that's evident in nasty politics, dystopian entertainment and the dissatisfaction many Americans feel with, well, practically everything. This is what happens when you get caught in the Liberty Trap, which is why breaking out of the trap—through individual action rather than the mirage of government solutions—is the best hope we have for an American revival and the rekindling of the freedoms we cherish.

SIX

THE MYTH OF THE
RUGGED INDIVIDUALIST

DO A WEB SEARCH FOR THE WORDS *SURVIVES WIL-derness*. If you want to get fancy, begin with *man, woman, boy, girl* or *mother-in-law*. What you'll inevitably find is the latest breathless tale of something that seems remarkable these days: a human being emerging alive from a terrifying brush with nature. The last time I did that Web search, a story popped up about a 67-year-old guy who ran out of gas in a remote corner of Washington state and spent a week in his pickup truck, surviving on Snickers bars and rainwater, until a bow hunter stumbled across him.[1]

Now, briefly transport yourself back to America's early days. Imagine getting lost in the woods for a week or so and living to tell the tale. Would your ordeal seem heroic? Would the newspapers write about it? Would everybody gather round at the ale house as you described how you ate bugs to survive and fended off wildlife? Doubtful. Surviving the wilderness was an everyday part of life for many people two or three centuries ago, especially if you were a trapper, logger, soldier, surveyor or other type of tradesman who made a living in the untamed outdoors. One of George Washington's early adventures, at the age of 21, was a 250-mile trip on horseback from Virginia to northeastern Pennsylvania in the winter of 1753 to scout out French settlements on behalf of rival British interests. "The whole face of the earth was covered with snow and the waters with ice," Washington wrote later. There were no roads and often no trails, forcing Washington's party to slash their way through dense forest. They rode their horses through frigid rivers and were wet much of the time. Oh yeah, Washington also had to make peace with various Indian tribes along the way, or risk getting slaughtered.[2]

The way we define liberty today derives from the way the United States was founded and the sensibilities of the founders. Life, liberty and the pursuit of happiness were principal aims laid out in the Declaration of Independence, after all. Yet we can be bad historians, oversimplifying what happened in the past and selectively recalling events that support our point of view while repressing those that don't. In many ways, we distort America's founding narrative to justify a kind of personal entitlement that was not, in fact, part of the founding ethos of the nation.

We tend to see the founding fathers in ourselves, as if Washington or Jefferson or Madison would slap us on the back if they materialized in the current day and congratulate us on being such terrific caretakers of the liberties they enshrined. It's debatable whether they would feel that way. For one thing, we enjoy privileges that were literally unimaginable back then—and we haven't necessarily harnessed those privileges to further the cause of liberty. Modern medicine didn't exist in George Washington's day, when many procedures, such as bloodletting to drain dangerous humors from the body, were more likely to cause harm than anything. Yet for all our medical advantages today, Americans suffer from obesity, diabetes, heart disease and other ailments at rates that probably would have astonished and alarmed the founders.

Leisure time is another modern privilege that was unknown to ordinary people back then; there were no labor-saving household gizmos like dishwashers and laundry machines, or even electricity. But what have we done with that found time? Invented television, celebrities, video games, cat slide shows and many other amusements that keep us entertained but don't really improve living standards or help anybody get ahead. Financial panics were common and ruinous back then, and ordinary people had no access to insurance, government benefits or other types of safety nets, except maybe whatever support family and friends could offer in a pinch. If you failed, you dug yourself out and started over, lest ye perish. We have many more safeguards against disaster today, yet those protections have arguably made us more risk-averse, less motivated, and addicted to comfort at the expense of ambition. It's worth asking whether the founders would applaud or weep if they fell out of the sky into a modern mall or living room—once they adjusted to self-flushing toilets and microwave popcorn.

We think of the founders and the origins of America the way we want to understand them rather than the way they really were. Since our modern conception of liberty puts an emphasis on individual rights, for instance, we tend to think that's how the founders thought when they were molding the nation and writing the Constitution. It's not. The word *individualist* wasn't even in common usage back then. The founders worried about putting too much emphasis on individual rights, not too little. George Washington had been appalled at the selfishness of the citizenry when he commanded the Continental Army, as war contractors, politicians and even some of his soldiers continually pursued their own private interests at the expense of the revolutionary cause.[3] James Madison was particularly skeptical of individuals' ability to govern themselves effectively. At the Constitutional Convention in 1787, the founders were "extraordinarily fearful of any kind of rule by the people," says legal scholar Sanford Levinson. "They really didn't have any confidence in citizens."[4] When they had finally drafted the Constitution we hold in reverence today, a woman saw Ben Franklin in the street and asked him, "Well, Doctor, what have we got? A republic or a monarchy?" "A republic," Franklin famously answered, "if you can keep it."[5]

Even basic words had a different meaning then than they do now. Think about "life, liberty and the pursuit of happiness," perhaps the most enduring phrase from the Declaration of Independence. What does that mean to you? A good job and comfortable retirement, maybe? A nice house, clean car, overstuffed couch, flat-screen TV? Afternoons on the golf course or tennis courts or loafing on an overstuffed chaise? The authors of the Declaration of Independence had a different idea. "When the founders wrote about life, liberty, and the pursuit of happiness," says historian David Halberstam, "they didn't mean longer vacations and more comfortable hammocks. They meant the pursuit of learning. The love of learning. The pursuit of improvement and excellence."[6] Suddenly the founders no longer seem

to be endorsing a smartphone in every pocket, an SUV in every driveway or a check from the government whenever you run short. Maybe
they had something else in mind.

As for the Constitution itself, the founders were less impressed
by their own handiwork than we are today. Thomas Jefferson believed any constitution ought to expire after 19 years, because "if it be
enforced longer, it is an act of force not of right."[7] As proof of that,
the original Constitution had several deep flaws, as is well known.
It sanctioned slavery, only allowed property owners to vote and gave
men more rights than women—provisions that were eventually over-
turned as the public understanding of liberty became more expansive.
In January 2011, members of the newly seated 112th Congress read
the Constitution aloud on the floor of the House of Representatives
as a sign of their fealty to it—but omitted the portions referring to
slavery, generating a controversy that overshadowed the whole pious
event.[8] "It's often noted that the United States is governed by the
world's oldest written constitution that is still in use," legal journalist Jeffrey Toobin has noted. "This is usually stated as praise, though
most other products of the 18th century, like horse-borne travel and
leech-based medical treatment, have been replaced by improved
models."[9]

The rugged individual is somebody we think of as the quintessential American, but that's not how early Americans thought of
themselves. They were rugged by necessity because that's how everybody lived back then. Later generations crafted the rugged individualist motif as they tried to describe what makes America different
and special. There was at least a little mythmaking involved in that, a
tradition, needless to say, that still flourishes today. In modern times,

evoking the rugged American individualist is usually a ploy by marketers to sell jeans or SUVs or cigarettes, or by politicians to flatter voters and thereby get elected.

The meme of the rugged individualist who prizes personal liberty above all began to take shape in the 1830s, when Henry Clay, the congressman and presidential candidate from Kentucky, started to use the phrase "self-made men." In the "American System" speech he gave in the Senate in 1832, Clay declared, "In Kentucky, almost every manufactory known to me is in the hands of enterprising self-made men, who have acquired whatever wealth they possess by patient and diligent labor."[10] Here's something that will help differentiate the past from the present: Clay's speech was so long that the original text ran for 32 pages spaced more tightly than a cheap Bible, and it took him three days to deliver the whole thing. The part about self-made men was buried more than halfway through, and it didn't exactly make the headlines the following day. But Clay's idea recalled the quintessential American hero, Ben Franklin, who did in fact spring from humble beginnings and built a personal franchise out of wit, charm, ingenuity and industriousness. "A Plowman on his Legs is higher than a Gentleman on his Knees," Franklin wrote, in the persona of Poor Richard, voicing the Everyman's pride that would eventually become an American hallmark.[11]

When Clay evoked Franklin in his lengthy Senate speech, America was no longer reeling from war debts or other start-up costs, which had persisted for decades after the Revolutionary War. It was beginning to prosper, as a nation of vast land and abundant natural resources should. The Industrial Revolution was kicking into gear, and a busy new mechanized society was beginning to displace the old agriculture-based economy. An emerging class of entrepreneurs was earning good money (and sometimes losing it more quickly than it arrived) from deal making, innovation and land speculation, instead of toiling for long hours on farms for scant daily wages. Young men were breaking with family tradition and leaving home to find their fortunes elsewhere. "Instead of following—and honoring—the traditional paths blazed by their parents and ancestors . . . these young innovators struck out on their own in a dramatic burst of individualism that carried significant risks but also promised substantial rewards," scholar Robert Bellah argues.[12]

So it's no surprise that others picked up on Clay's theme. Alexis de Tocqueville, the French intellectual who came to America in the 1830s and wrote several volumes on American society that came to be known as *Democracy in America*, informed his many readers in Europe that most wealthy Americans "were once poor; they have felt the sting of want; they were long a prey to adverse fortunes."[13] That was a revelation to the aristocrats who pulled most of the levers in the old world. Tocqueville seems to have been the one to coin the word *individualist* in order to describe the peculiar Americans he encountered. American individualism, the Frenchman explained, "is a mature and calm feeling, which disposes each member of the community to sever himself from the mass of his fellow-creatures; and to draw apart with his family and his friends; so that, after he has thus formed a little circle of his own, he willingly leaves society at large to itself."[14] Americans hearing that description of themselves might break out in cheering and back-slapping, but Tocqueville didn't mean it entirely as praise. Such a democracy, he said, "throws [every man] back forever upon himself alone, and threatens in the end to confine him entirely within the solitude of his own heart."[15] In civic matters, he warned, individualistic Americans were prone to "general apathy" that could result in abusive, unaccountable government.[16] Tocqueville's work is remarkable not just because he described America better than virtually any American of his time was able to do, but also because his observations seem as true today as ever.

Outspoken Americans had some trenchant observations of their own regarding the American character. In 1841, famed intellectual Ralph Waldo Emerson published a set of essays including a lecture he had been giving on the merits of self-reliance, which would draw cheers from conservative corners if published today. Emerson praised the simple, hearty man of "aboriginal strength," while decrying the "parlour soldiers" he saw all around him, who "shun the rugged battle of fate, where strength is born. . . . A sturdy lad from New Hampshire or Vermont," Emerson declared, "who in turn tries all the professions, who *teams it, farms it, peddles,* keeps a school, preaches, edits a newspaper, goes to Congress, buys a township, and so forth, in successive years, and always, like a cat, falls on his feet, is worth a hundred of these city dolls."[17] A few years later, Emerson's younger pal, Henry David Thoreau, went to "live deliberately" on wooded land Emerson owned near Walden Pond, south of Concord, Massachusetts, soon to publish the book that would brand him a pioneering environmentalist and rugged individualist.

America as a whole endorsed rugged individualism (though the phrase wasn't in vogue yet) when it elected Andrew Jackson in 1828. Jackson grew up poor on what was then the western frontier of the Carolinas—Daniel Boone's stomping ground several decades earlier— and received little schooling. He managed to pass the bar in North

Carolina and became a successful lawyer in Tennessee, mostly by going after debtors on behalf of wealthy landowners and other powerful people. During the War of 1812, Jackson was an aggressive military commander who crushed the Creek Indians—who were allied with the British—in Georgia and Alabama and defeated a British garrison in New Orleans, making him a war hero. Recalled to military duty in 1817, Jackson ordered an invasion of Florida in response to sporadic unrest there, a controversial move that nonetheless helped speed the United States' acquisition of Florida from Spain. The 1828 election made Jackson the first "western" president, the first born into poverty and the first to win through a populist strategy aimed directly at voters instead of through the workings of established political machinery. His reelection in 1832—the same year Clay paid homage to the self-made American—proved that Jackson's rough-hewn individualism had lasting appeal, as it still does today.

His presidency didn't exactly have a happy ending, though. Jackson pursued a "sound money" policy during his second term that included, among other things, a requirement that public lands be purchased with gold or silver rather than paper currency. He also effectively killed the Second Bank of the United States, a precursor to the Federal Reserve that demagogues and statists opposed on the grounds that it favored corporate interests and government bureaucrats over the common man. Yet it was the common man who suffered most when Jackson's economic policies led to the Panic of 1837, a grueling depression characterized by plunging land values, widespread business failures and a chaotic currency situation. By then, Jackson had left office, leaving his successors to deal with the costs of what, to him, was enhanced freedom.

In 1872, famous orator and diplomat Frederick Douglass gave a speech devoted to the many wonders of self-made men, which by then had become a familiar American trope. His words connect the rumblings of 1776 to many attributes still popular today. "America," Douglass declared, "is said, and not without reason, to be preeminently the home and patron of self-made men. . . . Self-made men are the men who, under peculiar difficulties and without the ordinary helps of favoring circumstances, have attained knowledge, usefulness, power and position and have learned from themselves the best uses to which life can be put in this world. . . . They are the men who owe little or nothing to birth, relationship, friendly surroundings; to wealth inherited or to early approved means of education."[18] Around the same time, Horatio Alger began to publish his simplistic tales of "Ragged Dick" and other up-from-the-gutter heroes, ultimately numbering more than 100 novels. Though almost laughably treacly, Alger's tales clearly appealed to an audience eager to be inspired; they sold more than 20 million copies.

There was undoubtedly some truth to the idea of a nation of ingenious, determined upstarts. Yet behind the pronouncements of these eighteenth-century image makers was a fair bit of showmanship. Henry Clay, while giving a name to the industriousness he so admired in his fellow Americans, wasn't exactly self-made himself. He was born into a moderately wealthy family able to pay for him to study law, and he married up in his early 20s, coming into enough money to own a 600-acre Kentucky estate by the time he was 35. Emerson's exhortations have guided the lives, or at least the attitudes, of many individualists and nonconformists since he uttered them, yet there was also a callous edge to some of his proclamations. "Do not tell me, as a good man did to-day, of my obligation to put all poor men in good situations," he grumped in one essay. Some critics, in fact, have charged that Emerson's focus on the self was more like narcissism than self-reliance.[19]

Then there's Abraham Lincoln, whom Douglass praised as "the King of American self-made men." "This man," Douglass said in his famous speech, "came to us, not from the schools or from the mansions of ease and luxury, but from the back woods." That may be more or less true, but some Lincoln scholars detect a self-serving impulse in the tale of humble origins that Lincoln himself repeated time and again. "Lincoln self-consciously grounded his entire political career within the context of a personal triumph over inherited adversity," historian and Lincoln biographer Kenneth J. Winkle explains.[20] By some accounts, Lincoln's self-made image was a shrewdly honed myth that Lincoln used shamelessly to further his own political career. He did leave home to make a better life for himself—a key distinction of nineteenth-century American entrepreneurs—but he also preferred mental labor over physical work. At a young age he learned the value of lowering expectations, then impressing onlookers by exceeding them. The image molding was part of Lincoln's genius: He fashioned himself the archetypal American while the form itself was still taking shape.

By the 1890s, America as a nation was more than a century old, and it had grown from a prodigious if awkward upstart into a strutting and powerful arriviste. It was now possible to connect the traits that seemed uniquely American with the runaway success that would make the United States the world's richest and perhaps most ambitious nation. Reflecting on all this, historian Frederick Jackson Turner wrote in 1893 that it was the existence of the frontier—first at the edge of the Atlantic, when early European settlers sailed west, then ever westward over land as the nation expanded—that gave America its special character. "To the frontier," he wrote, "the American intellect owes its striking characteristics. That coarseness and strength combined with acuteness and inquisitiveness, that practical, inventive turn of mind, quick to find expedients, that masterful grasp of material things, lacking in the artistic but powerful to effect great ends, that restless, nervous energy, that dominant individualism, working for good and for evil, and withal that buoyancy and exuberance which comes with freedom—these are traits of the frontier."[21]

Turner identified the frontier mentality that seemed to make America a land of bold adventurists. Yet there's another way of looking at the frontier that's not nearly so buoyant or exuberant. Michael Kimmel, a sociologist at Stony Brook University in New York, characterizes the westward migration of Americans during the 1800s not as some kind of heroic quest, but as "the westward expansion of losers." Anybody who became successful on the East Coast, Kimmel argues, was unlikely to leave for a high-risk life of privation and danger. "If you succeed and make a name for yourself in New York, then you stay there," he says. "But if you don't, then you try Chicago. If that doesn't work out, you go to Denver. No luck? It's off to Sacramento." The frontier, in that view, offered an escape to people who couldn't live up to the self-made standard and gave them a chance to try again, hopefully with better odds.[22] It's also worth keeping in mind that what drew many migrants to the woolly, unsettled West was the offer of free land under the Homestead Act of 1862—a program that might be considered a government handout today.

Even Turner recognized the dangers of a frontier mentality that prized individualism over the more communal attitudes of Europe. "The democracy born of free land, strong in selfishness and individualism, intolerant of administrative experience and education, and pressing individual liberty beyond its proper bounds, has its dangers as well as its benefits," he wrote. "Individualism in America has allowed a laxity in regard to governmental affairs which has rendered possible the spoils system and all the manifest evils that follow from the lack of a highly developed civic spirit."[23]

Nonetheless, the mythic heroism of the rugged individualist had been hatched and nourished. All that was needed was the name itself, which materialized in 1928 in a speech given by Herbert Hoover, of all people. Hoover gained notoriety as the president who flailed his way through the first three years of the Great Depression and left the White House in 1933 bewildered and defeated. But for most of his career in business and politics, he had been a wunderkind who succeeded at almost everything he tried. He lost both parents as a child, grew up in the home of an aunt and uncle, graduated with the first class at Stanford, became a renowned engineer and businessman, and amassed a $4 million fortune—more than $90 million today—by the time he was 40. He was the epitome of Henry Clay's self-made man. While running for president in 1928, he gave a speech defining what, to him, made America different from everywhere else— especially Europe, which was still reeling in the aftermath of World War I. He described the difference between the "American system of rugged individualism and a European philosophy . . . of paternalism and state socialism." Had America mimicked Europe, he insisted, "it would have meant the undermining of the individual initiative and enterprise through which our people have grown to unparalleled greatness."[24] Hoover's appeal to the rugged individualist helped him win the presidency that November, and while Hoover would soon become a casualty of the Depression, the rugged individual he created lives on as a sort of ideal to which Americans aspire both consciously and unwittingly. Marketers for decades have helped us express our rugged individualism through products such as Marlboro cigarettes, Levi's and Wrangler jeans, Jeep vehicles, NASCAR auto racing and hundreds of other things we can buy as a show of solidarity with eighteenth- and nineteenth-century outdoorsmen. The rugged individualist is a focal point of virtually every national political campaign, with candidates of both parties lauding his virtues and seeking his vote. He even stars in reality shows such as *Duck Dynasty*, mesmerizing an audience that seemingly can't believe anybody still hunts bullfrogs for dinner and literally earns a living off the land. Beyond the superficial appeal, however, is a message about self-reliance many of us may be straining to hear. The rugged individualist has become a trope, an almost fictional character. Something seems to be telling us to breathe fresh life into him. To animate him. To survive a brush with nature or some other type of intimidating ordeal and emerge strengthened rather than weakened.

SEVEN

DEPENDENCY AUDIT

IN 1959, ETHEL ANDRUS, WHO FOUNDED THE AMERI-can Association of Retired Persons (AARP), insisted that the group would never "bewail the hardships of old age . . . nor stress the potential political strength of older folk, nor urge governmental subsidy." As if to amplify that, the White House Conference on Aging in 1961 declared that "the individual will assume the primary responsibility for self-reliance in old age." Yet Medicare and other Great Society programs became law just a few years later, and a new generation quickly got used to the idea of government-funded health care for the elderly and a lot of other subsidies for both the poor and the middle class. By the 1970s, AARP had totally flip-flopped. "You've already paid most of your dues," its brochures reminded members. "Now start collecting the benefits." In less than 20 years, America had morphed from a nation that emphasized self-reliance in both word and deed to one that paid lip service to self-reliance while feasting on the new notion of entitlement. Today, a majority of Americans—of all ages—support entitlement programs for seniors. And AARP has become a formidable lobbying group that routinely harnesses the political strength of older folk and fiercely protects governmental subsidies for its members.[1]

There's nothing inherently wrong with taxpayer-funded subsidy programs voters approve for themselves. Medicare and Social Security might be exactly the type of hedge against poverty a wealthy nation ought to provide its senior citizens, rather than counting on private charities or neighborly goodwill to handle the burden. The problem comes when sustenance from elsewhere dulls the instincts needed to provide it yourself. In his famous speech extolling self-made men, Frederick Douglass warned of the "favoring conditions" that can erode self-reliance. "If you wish to make your son helpless," Douglass said, "you need not cripple him with bullet or bludgeon, but simply place him beyond the reach of necessity and surround him with ease and luxury. . . . Where circumstances do most for men, there man will do least for himself."[2] By the beginning of the twenty-first century, the insidious ramifications of ease and luxury that Douglass warned about had seeded themselves throughout American society.

The unprecedented creation of wealth from 1950 to 1980, which flatlined but stayed more or less steady for another 20 years, fostered the flowering of individualism without the ruggedness that had traditionally accompanied it. The leathery, go-it-alone cowboy who was a cultural hero of the 1950s and early 1960s gave way to the counterculture antiheroes of the late 1960s and 1970s. "If you want to sing out, sing out," Cat Stevens sang, "and if you want to be free, be free."[3]

Like many things that evoke liberty, that song later turned up in a TV commercial, helping T-Mobile sell smartphones.

In the 1980s, pop philosopher Joseph Campbell urged baby boomers to "follow your bliss."[4] One of them, Steve Jobs, followed that advice by helping create the anticorporate corporation, Apple Computer. Apple announced its intention to shatter conventional thinking in a 1984 Super Bowl commercial in which a female athlete hurled a sledgehammer into a video screen broadcasting an image of an Orwellian cult leader.[5] This wasn't the frontier individualism of Andrew Jackson and Abraham Lincoln or even the imagined toughness of John Wayne. It was a new kind of individualism enabled by "pervasive affluence," according to historian Neil Howe.[6] The freedoms that accompanied this affluence weren't earned through self-reliance, but almost through the opposite—institutional strength that lifted the living standards of nearly all Americans.

Living standards have continued to improve, though perhaps more slowly and sporadically. We have bigger homes, safer cars and more amusements today than we know what to do with. We have better health care, far more access to information, smartphone apps that change the thermostat and monitor our bank accounts, and even the ability to skip commercials on TV. At the same time, something is clearly wrong. The wealth that used to stay in America now floods everywhere because big US companies like Apple, Nike, General Motors and General Electric can make stuff wherever in the world they choose to and sell it overseas as well. The digital revolution may be even more disruptive, with microprocessors and the machines they power changing commerce and replacing workers faster than a lot of people can adapt. In the economy the baby boomers grew up in, a mainframe computer could last 30 years or more. These days, computing gizmos and the apps they run on can become outdated in a year or less, which has generated a rapid and relentless pace of change. Big economic shake-ups have occurred before, and living standards have always resumed their upward climb after a period of disruption. It's that period of disruption that's the problem—and we're in that period now. Millions of families are being disrupted, and their financial freedom is suffering.

The conditions many middle- and lower-income families find themselves in today rank somewhere between curious and alarming, depending on whom you ask. Economist Gary Shilling estimates that nearly 60 percent of the US population is dependent on government for a major portion of their income, a figure that includes not just beneficiaries of government programs but also bureaucrats, soldiers, teachers and others whose pay comes at least in part from taxpayer funds.[7] Meanwhile, the portion of adult Americans who belong to the labor force—which means they're either working or looking for work—has been declining, especially the percentage of men between the ages of 30 and 49. Government disability benefits have become a primary source of income for 14 million people. In some areas, 25 percent of the population receives disability, with banks and stores staying open late on the one day each month when government checks arrive.[8] "These numbers have no precedent," says scholar Charles Murray, "in a country where, until the last few decades, it was taken for granted that all adult males in the prime of life who were not completely disabled would be working or looking for work."[9] Compare that with this observation from Francis Grund, a German writer who sailed across the Atlantic and wrote about American culture around the same time

Tocqueville did. "I have never known a native American to ask for charity," Grund observed. "An American, embarrassed by his pecuniary circumstances, can hardly be prevailed upon to ask or accept the assistance of his own relations; and will, in many instances, scorn to have recourse to his own parents."[10]

Conservatives see these trends as moral rot ruining everything. Liberals argue that crony capitalism has enriched a tiny portion of the population at the expense of everybody else. The whole tired argument plays out ad nauseam in Washington, DC, while all across America, partisans on either side lap it up—and the Liberty Trap clamps down on them. Yes, the nation's leaders should be fostering new ways for America to capitalize on its innate advantages, fix what's broken and generate more prosperity for everybody. They're not, and we all know the infuriating story. But if you think political solutions are the only solutions, you haven't taken a close enough look at your own portfolio of choices.

Like many Americans, I'd like to think of myself as a rugged individualist. I could fake it and pretend it's true, yet Superstorm Sandy proved I'm fooling myself. And the things I consider rugged in the first place are actually aided to a large extent by machines, infrastructure and other people's innovations and hard work. When I go skiing, I pay a considerable amount of money to ride a mechanical lift up the mountain, then sachet down a trail that's been cut through the trees for my benefit. Even though I can change the oil in my car, I hate the feel of it on my fingers, which is why I go to Jiffy Lube instead. I'd split my own firewood except it makes my back sore. I have to exercise in a gym because the work I do for a living, as a writer, only burns about 11 calories per day. I even developed a repetitive-stress injury in my arm from using a computer mouse at the wrong angle. George Washington would be baffled.

One of the questions that led to this book is how well I'd be able to survive if many of the necessities I take for granted were suddenly unavailable. Before I went out in the woods to test my mettle with the New York City Preppers, I constructed a dependency audit to assess how much I really rely on things beyond my control. When I was younger and precynical, if you had asked me to rate my personal freedom on a scale of 1 to 10, I probably would have said 8. As a journalist, I enjoy the protections of the First Amendment nearly every day. I've mostly made all my own choices in life, including a few I wish somebody had talked me out of. Still, they were my choices, and freedom includes the freedom to be a fool. The only reason I wouldn't have rated my freedom a 9 or 10 is I lack the wealth and audacity to truly do everything I want, which is probably a good thing.

But my thinking has changed on account of the 2008 financial meltdown, a warming planet we're doing nothing about, corrupt crony capitalism in much of the Western world (the liberals are sorta right), and a mushrooming welfare state (the conservatives are sorta right, too). I'm also one of the baby busters who assumes Social Security and Medicare will be bankrupt by the time I'm old enough to enroll, which means I'm paying into a system that may never pay me back. At a younger age, writing off government retirement benefits is a kind of hip fatalism, as if you're too cool to care. As you get older, however, the idea that the government might be conducting a kind of Ponzi scheme—with your money—gets nettlesome.

For my dependency audit, I listed the things I do on a regular basis and grouped them into nine different types of dependencies.

Driving is something I do often, for example, and when I drive I'm dependent on roads being there, traffic lights keeping some kind of order, gas being available (if you can't tell, I suffer from postsuperstorm gasoline anxiety) and, scariest of all, competent drivers in all the other cars. For the most part, what I depend on when I drive is physical infrastructure, and there's virtually nothing I can do to create that on my own. So in order to drive, I'm highly dependent on the existence of something I can't really control. The same goes with placing a phone call (since I don't know how to build my own phone or run phone lines to Pittsburgh, where my mom lives), watching TV (it would be too hard to create my own programming) and buying a new refrigerator or furnace (you get the idea). But I'm not dependent on others for everything. I could grow some of my own food if I wanted to, I can cut my hair myself instead of going to a barber and I can build a large network of friends or a small one—it's pretty much up to me.

On the next page are the nine types of dependencies I discovered, along with my own assessment of how dependent I am in each category.

In four of nine categories, I rated myself fairly or highly dependent, with a score of either 4 or 5. That basically means I couldn't function normally without people or things I have no control over. I'm somewhat dependent (a score of 3) in four other categories—professional services, financial wherewithal, good health and chance—because there are some things I can do on my own to get what I need or improve my standing. The only category in which I'm relatively independent (score of 2) is community, since I can choose whether to be socially active and to get involved in organized activities or not. In

NINE CATEGORIES OF THINGS I'M DEPENDENT UPON

Dependency	Examples	Types of Dependent Activities	Dependency Level: 1 = least, 5 = most
Physical infrastructure	Power grid, roads, airports, stores	Driving, shopping, turning on heat, A/C, lights or water	5
Electronic infrastructure	Internet, cellular networks, cable TV	Using email, surfing the Web, using smartphone, working	4
Professional services	Insurers, banks, lawyers, vets, barbers, people I work with	Buying auto and home insurance, shopping, personal grooming, working	3
Manufactured goods	Car, computer, smartphone, appliances, clothes, pet food	Driving, watching TV, using computer, cooking	4
Social order	Traffic lights, lines at delis, respect for social customs, law and order	Feeling safe at home and in public, moving around efficiently	4
Community	Family, friends, life partner, opportunities to meet new people	Visiting with family, going out to dinner, going to parties, sports leagues, church if religious	2
Good health	Illness, disease, physical condition, genetics	Eating well or poorly, working out or not, preventive medicine	3
Financial wherewithal	Money and the freedom to spend it as desired	Shopping, taking vacations, affording health care and education, planning for retirement	3
Chance	Safety, avoiding accidents, finding opportunity	Work, enjoying leisure, enjoying family . . . everything	3

NOTE: Most activities involve more than one type of dependency.

none of the nine categories can I award myself a score of 1, claiming to be truly independent.

Other people, needless to say, might rate their own dependency differently, but I'll bet there are several commonalities most of us share. First, most people are highly dependent on technology because they have no idea how to build most of the things we rely on every day. In the 1980s, the Nobel Prize–winning economist Milton Friedman popularized an old story entitled "I, Pencil," which described the many things that must happen all over the world to enable production of an ordinary pencil: Wood must come from felled trees in the Pacific Northwest, then shipped to a mill with machinery itself refined from dozens of different ores and other materials from who knows where, until wood slats of exact dimensions are wrapped around "lead" that comes from a graphite mine in Ceylon, and that subcomponent is then topped by a ferrule made of brass and then the obligatory eraser, both of which have their own complex lineages.[11] Today, a pencil seems like such a primitive tool that it's almost like some kind of prehistoric leftover. But I couldn't make one. Could you? And if you can't make a pencil, how would you get by without somebody else building the technology that enables credit cards, email, smartphones, apps and, dare I add, TV?

Second, health almost deserves to be a special category, because it can have an outsized effect on how dependent or self-sufficient you are. If you're healthy, you're free of a byzantine medical system that can be an affliction in itself. If you're sick, you're a prisoner of the most complicated and expensive health-care industry in the history of the free world. Healthy is definitely the way to go. It allows you to invest in a business or finance education for your kids instead of blowing your life savings on two days of hospital care. By one simple measure, people who exercise regularly—one determinant of good health—earn 9 percent more than those who don't.[12] Being healthy enables many of the things that help us get ahead, such as performing well at our jobs, multitasking and being socially engaged. And there are some things we can do to safeguard our health, such as eating well, exercising, wearing a seat belt and getting checkups on schedule. Yet many people don't bother, which is an astonishing forfeiture of freedom. Maybe it's no coincidence that dependency in America has risen to record highs by some measures at the same time there's an epidemic of obesity and other preventable health problems.

Third, I noticed that the types of activities that make me feel most independent tend to be ones that rely on community rather than technology, infrastructure or stuff produced in a factory. Socializing, spending time with family, participating in community events and forming relationships are activities for which I gave myself a high self-sufficiency rating, and they're also things we can typically do without computers, roads, subscriptions, memberships or government regulation. All you really need is people, which for better or worse are generally in ample supply.

Finally, luck is a huge factor in self-sufficiency. In each of the four categories in which I gave myself a rating of 2 or 3, it's partly because I am lucky—to be healthy, to have been born into a stable family, to have received a good education, to have the ability to improve my own prospects and to have avoided outright calamity (so far). There are some things we can do to make ourselves a bit more lucky since fortune favors the prepared mind, as Louis Pasteur famously said.

But for the most part, luck is random, which means at least part of self-sufficiency is, too.

Nonetheless, conducting a dependency audit made me feel less free than I used to feel, and instead of an 8, I now rated my personal liberty a 5 or a 6. Pretty middling. There were simply too many things that would leave me bumbling around if they went wrong. I was much more rugged in my own mind than in reality. The time had finally come to test just how rugged I was, and whether it was possible to become more so.

EIGHT

PREPPER MOUNTAIN

FOR SOME REASON, ON THAT FIRST NIGHT OF THE Tough Preppers' Bug-Out Weekend, we finished the soggy, cold evening talking about brown recluse spiders, which, as Omar—a bottomless font of helpful, practical knowledge—eagerly insisted, are indigenous to the Catskill region, where we were, and are quite unassuming until they've bitten you and you notice your flesh begins to decompose, right there on your arm or leg.[1] Suddenly, everybody had a brown recluse story to share, right before bedtime. Unlike the distinctive black widow, I learned, with its red hourglass tattoo that glows like a beacon, the brown recluse's violin-shaped marking is hard to spot, especially in the dark. You may never even notice that one of these spiders has bitten you until a few hours later, when a sinkhole forms in your flesh. And oh yeah, the brown recluse loves to take refuge in sleeping bags, especially when it's cold outside.

The regrettable moment came when we could no longer kill time next to the fire and had to repair to our tents for a night of "sleep." Jason Charles, the New York City firefighter who organized the weekend, had planned to call for volunteers to pull guard duty for two-hour shifts all night long since we were simulating a disaster in which marauders eager to seize all our tools and supplies might be lurking like the Viet Cong just outside our camp perimeter. But given the rain and miserable conditions, he decided to call that off, stirring relief among—well, me. So I sloshed over to my tent with my half-numb hands in my half-burned gloves, eager to close my eyes and wait for time to pass while I fantasized about being on my couch at home and not caring at all whether I was rugged or utterly helpless.

I was out with the preppers, you may recall, to test how rugged my individualism was. Self-reliance is one of the five endangered freedoms, so the idea was to learn how to make myself more independent. So far, my list of ruggedization tips included: DON'T FREEZE TO DEATH and BRING WATERPROOF GLOVES. I didn't think I would actually die of cold that first night since I had read of people getting stuck deep in the wilderness during the winter and surviving by building an igloo, eating snow, and spooning with people like Omar to conserve body heat. I figured I could get a lot of heat from Omar if I really had to. But what those survival memoirs don't usually convey is the regret and stupidity you feel at having made yourself so uncomfortable, and the fact that you would probably just give up if you could. As I shivered, my desire to become more rugged went numb, because ruggedness was turning out to be a real pain in the ass.

Another survival tip I suddenly learned: START PRACTICING YOGA, because squeezing into my narrow one-person tent turned out to be a trick for contortionists. After an awkward struggle to get my boots off in the front porch area of my tent, where they'd be sheltered from the rain but zipped out of the sleeping compartment, I managed to wriggle into my sleeping bag and maneuver my inflatable sleeping pad and pillow into position. I was doing all this with a miners-style headlamp strapped to my forehead, which might sound goofy but is indispensable when you need both hands to move stuff around in the dark. Just as I was beginning to get marginally comfortable, I glanced at the wall of my tent and suddenly felt like I was in a Godzilla movie. The silhouette of a spider, as big as my head, was perched on the wall, as if inspecting my exposed neck for the best place to pounce. I had been worried about a petite little brown recluse getting into my sleeping bag, and here, Arachnosaurus Rex was hanging out in my tent. I practically rolled my tent over when I tried to leap away from the ferocious beast, but as I jerked around I noticed the image of the spider jerked around, too. Then it dawned on me: Something had alighted on my headlamp, which was projecting a magnified image of the creature onto the tent wall. I tore off the headlamp and sure enough, there was a smallish and, unfortunately, brown spider sitting on it, and when I glanced upward, I saw a few of his pals moseying along the top of my tent, only 18 inches or so above my head. No doubt they were just waiting for me to turn the lights off, so they could Spidey down their webs into my sleeping bag for a cozy night of slumber and flesh gnawing. I resisted the urge to examine these critters too closely, lest they display the dreaded violin-shaped mark of the devil. What would I do if I spotted it? Burn the tent and spend the night standing in the rain? Ask Omar to share his sleeping quarters? Better, I figured, to squish every spider I could find in a tissue I pulled from my pack, and, if I missed one or two, hope for the best. Had you seen my tent from the outside as I came to terms with this spider infestation and probed every corner for invaders, you might have thought an orgy was going on in there. Minus the pleasant sounds.

Usually, when I find an unwelcome pest at home, I usher it outside, doing my best not to upset Mother Nature. In the tent, however, it was too hard to spin myself around to reach the tent flap while keeping an eye on the spiders. It was a cage match between me and the spiders, so after squishing them, I wrapped the carcasses in tissue and placed them in a corner that was easy to reach, about a foot from my head. The karma was terrible, but it had been terrible since my gloves first got wet. Somehow, this would toughen me up.

There are some nights that surprise you simply because they end. It wasn't just the dead spiders that kept me awake all night. I had cleverly staked my tent on top of a tree root that seemed invisible when you walked over it but felt as big as a boulder when you tried to sleep on it. Unlike the real preppers, I hadn't brought a tarp to lay under my tent to insulate it from the cold, wet ground. The tent was supposedly waterproof, yet condensation formed on the inside, dripping onto my sleeping bag like a contraption for watering houseplants when you go on vacation. And even though I wore every layer I had brought, my shoulders felt naked, as if I had just emerged from a frigid plunge with those crazy "polar bear" winter swimmers you see on the Internet.

It surprised me, therefore, when I opened my eyes and noticed the darkness wasn't so dark any more. Eventually I crawled out of the tent to look for gaping flesh wounds in the daylight and found none. Then, a minor victory: Jason had managed to revive the fire, and I actually made a cup of coffee in my drinking tin, with grounds I had prewrapped in filters and tied off into single-serve portions, adding Splenda and powdered French vanilla creamer for that genuine, artificially flavored aromatic goodness. It had to be the best cup of coffee in the entire woods that morning—plus, I had finally accomplished something rugged, by making coffee without a coffeepot or even a stove.

A TV crew arrived around 9 a.m. We had been expecting them. A new season of *Doomsday Preppers* was about to start, and the *PBS NewsHour* decided to investigate whether real preppers were as crazy as those on the show. The crew had actually been there the day before, getting some priceless footage of Jason Charles marching up the mountain in a wife-beater tank top, muscles bulging and tattoos gleaming, with a monstrous pack on his back and that fearsome axe in one hand. Had they been able to beam that footage in real-time to all the hikers and campers within a 25-mile radius, there probably would have been a mass exodus out of the woods as people panicked over an armed marauder from Harlem. Unlike the preppers, the PBS crew repaired to a hotel for the evening, returning to the mountain the following day to pick up the story.

They arrived a bit late; most of the preppers had wandered out of their tents by the time the crew arrived. So the producer asked some of the preppers if they would mind going back into their tents and coming out again, so the crew could get footage of the preppers "waking up." (Spend a little time around a TV crew and you will *never* believe anything you see on the screen.) Being agreeable sorts,

the preppers complied. Then the crew began doing one-on-one interviews with various members of the group to find out what the heck
they were doing there.

As the crew teed up Omar, I sidled over to have a listen. "What
are you doing to prepare for a doomsday scenario?" the producer
asked him.

"Nothing," Omar replied, disappointing the producer. He wasn't
worried about the apocalypse, he explained. His real concern was
some kind of emergency that might generate civil unrest that would
spill out of New York City into his neighborhood, which was between
the Lincoln Tunnel and the George Washington Bridge in New Jersey, two of the main outlets for people who would flee Manhattan if
they really had to. If something like that ever happened, Omar's plan
was to walk 16 miles to his brother's house, which was a safer remove
from the frenzied commuting zones, and then use his prepper skills
to figure out what to do next.

"Are you worried about a financial collapse?" the producer asked.

"I don't have any money," Omar said, "so why do I care about
that? All I care about is a few pennies I have in the bank. I hope
those don't disappear." Omar turned out to be a tougher interview
on camera than I had guessed he would be. That was because the
producer was trying to bait Omar into being more of a fanatic than
he really was.

That became a recurring theme of the interviews. Al and Annette, who had gotten lost in the woods the night before, ended up
sleeping in their minivan at the bottom of the mountain and starting out again in the morning. With the aid of daylight, they found
the campsite with no problem, rolling in right around the time the

PBS crew did. Al told the PBS interviewer he wasn't worried about a doomsday scenario, either. "What I'm concerned about is, What happens if we lose our jobs?" he said. "We have food set aside but want to be more ready than that. I might be able to get another job, but when that will happen, we just don't know."

"I'm more concerned about a hurricane or a blackout," Annette chimed in.

Teli, the New Jersey contractor, was worried about another storm like Sandy, and he had researched how people in New Orleans in 2005 survived Hurricane Katrina, which was really two disasters—the natural one followed by a disorganized and chaotic relief effort. "It amazes me," he said, "when you ask people if they have a little bit of food and supplies stored away, and they say 'no, no we don't.' Why not? What's so hard about that?"

Superstorm Sandy also convinced Jodi and her boyfriend, Joe—soon to be dubbed the hipster preppers—that they needed to get more serious about surviving an urban meltdown. They had waited out Sandy in a comfortable apartment but also realized they might not be so lucky next time. "If they lock down the city, man, I don't want to be trapped in that fucking place," Joe said. "In my neighborhood"—Manhattan's Lower East Side—"they're gonna get their guns, get in packs and go crazy." The two of them were working on plans to escape New York City by foot if they had to—two of the people Omar was worried about showing up in his neighborhood, I guess.

But they would be bugging out in style. In her weekend bug-out bag, Jodi had brought mascara, a compact with a mirror, eye shadow, lipstick, concealer, eye cream and many other beauty aids. And to tell the truth, if you stumbled upon our group and needed to ask directions, you'd probably pass by me and the other disheveled, bedheaded campers and walk right up to Jodi, because she could easily have come right from a mall or restaurant. You would have preferred to eat with Jodi, too, because instead of freeze-dried camp food and granola bars, she and Joe had brought Italian tuna in olive oil with capers and lemon garlic, chicken sautéed in butter, grass-fed beef jerky, dried mango and a menuful of other delicacies, all organic. "We would have planned better meals," Jodi explained to me (off-camera), "except Joe said he wanted to rough it and eat tuna out of a can with his hands, like *Game of Thrones.*" Which Joe actually did.

The TV crew didn't pick up on it, but Jodi, despite her artful prepping, probably had the doomiest mentality of anybody in the group. At one point, she explained to the group that the world was controlled by a group of "global elites" who, among other things, keep people sick so they can reap billions selling pharmaceuticals. This cabal, she went on, cultivated illness as a form of population control while making sure true curatives—such as colloidal silver, oil of oregano, wheatgrass and manuka honey—remained discredited, hard-to-find substances never manufactured in quantities able to save a significant number of people. A few of the other preppers were familiar with this theory and tried to talk her out of it, but Jodi's intensity wore them down. Besides, the contents of her bug-out bag were more entertaining. When Jodi finished eating a container of lemon-caper Italian tuna and asked what she should do with the glass jar, Omar cackled as if she had asked where the bidet was. "A glass jar!" he chortled. "That's probably heavier than what was in it!" Jodi seemed to miss Omar's point, which was that when prepping for survival after a disaster, it's a good idea to pack light.

The TV crew wrapped up its work and headed back down the mountain. It's too bad the camera wasn't around to capture a few of the candid remarks that followed the crew's departure. "That PBS guy made a big deal about the axe," Jason groused. "It's for chopping wood. What the fuck do you think it's for? That whole doomsday thing. Man, get the fuck over it."

There was a broader agenda for the day than mugging for a TV camera. Jason taught us all a few survival skills, gleaned from his work as an EMT and a firefighter in New York City, plus other things he had picked up while researching prepping and simply testing his own ingenuity. There was reason to think the man knew what he was talking about. When we were hiking up the mountain together the day before, making small talk, I asked Jason how he had picked the site for the bug-out weekend. He told me he had researched a few different places, then come up with John, another prepper in our group, to reconnoiter the entire mountain in person—during a tropical storm. "That must have sucked," I said.

"Nah, it was okay," he answered.

"Seriously? You got stuck in a tropical storm and kept going?"

"We didn't get stuck in it," he explained. "We knew it was coming. We timed it so we'd be on the mountain during the storm. That's exactly the kind of thing we're prepping for. What better way to check out your gear?"

Well, I couldn't argue with that. I could argue with Jason's timing, I guess, but not with his logic.

Jason gave the group a primer on rough first aid, describing three different types of gash injuries: an ooze wound, a venous wound (into a vein) and an arterial wound, which is the kind that needs a tourniquet to prevent you from bleeding to death. The novices among us grew a bit queasy as Jason described the nauseating details of arterial wounds, especially if there's an angulated bone break to amplify the horror, known to laypeople as "the bone is sticking out." Jason must have noticed a few faces growing pale, because he stopped himself for a moment and then said, "Look, you gotta understand, these wounds are gonna hurt. You're just gonna have to deal with that. No one likes to hear other people scream. You're gonna have to suck it up. Get over the blood."

We learned how to make different types of lean-tos and emergency shelters out of sticks and leaves and whatever else might be lying around. Jason and a couple other preppers who knew what they were doing showed the rest of us how to use a compass to navigate through the woods, which is what you do, I guess, if your phone goes dead and you can't use your woodsman app. There was also a lot of informal information sharing, much as there had been at a couple of other afternoon prepper events I had attended before the big bug-out weekend.

Omar seemed to possess a lot of information that would probably be useless under normal circumstances—but might be invaluable in a real emergency. I imagined him to be a kind of mad genius of prepping. He was obviously intelligent, and as a kid he had gotten interested in mythology and folklore. "I wanted to be Indiana Jones," he said. But in Dominican families such as his, kids were expected to earn real money right away rather than indulging their interests by going to college. Omar got a GED high school equivalency degree and took a few college courses, but he made it to his current job as an IT project manager without ever getting a bachelor's degree.

Had I talked with Omar before outfitting my bug-out bag, I might have saved a couple hundred bucks and a fair amount of frustration. Omar confirmed what I had suspected—a considerable racket had sprung up around the business of selling people survival equipment. While doing my own research on bug-out gear, I had come across plenty of splashy magazine-style features detailing the contents of the "ultimate" bug-out bag, which inevitably included every conceivable gizmo for purifying water, summoning fire, trapping game and coaxing the medicinal properties out of plants—sometimes all-in-one. "Don't get so caught up in the gear," Omar advised. "A good bug-out bag is probably similar to a mountaineering bag from the 1970s. Go with the 10 essentials," which he explained were shelter, food, water, navigation, fire, a knife, cordage—"which for some reason has become a fancy word for rope"—and a few other basics. I had brought along a magnesium fire starter—hoping somebody would show me how to use it—along with stormproof matches and two or three other unconventional ways of starting a fire in case all the others failed. Unnecessary, Omar insisted: "Just bring three or four Bic lighters."

Since our group was entirely from New York City or the nearby area, everybody wanted to learn everything they could about ways to gain an edge if mayhem befell the city. Jason seemed to have a bit of the inside scoop from his work with the fire department. In a major emergency, he explained, the New York Police Department could have all the bridges and tunnels out of the city locked down within an hour, which could make it tricky to escape or even move around.

"Move at night," he advised. "Always assume somebody can see you. If you make yourself a target, people will know you've got something they want."

Somebody asked if it might make sense to hide in the subway tunnels. "The yellow hatches all over the city are service entrances to the subway," Omar helpfully volunteered. "They're supposed to be locked but somebody could forget and leave one open." An inconclusive discussion followed about the virtues of hoisting up a yellow hatch and ducking into a subway tunnel during an urban panic, and whether it would be worth battling New York's ubiquitous subway rats for territorial rights.

I spent the day continuing to learn small but vital lessons about self-reliance. I had purchased a water purification bottle so advanced it could filter out cholera and Ebola, from the sound of the claims on the packaging. Just one problem: After filling it up from a mountain stream, I couldn't get any water to come out of it, no matter how hard I sucked on the plastic straw. While I was complaining about what a piece of junk it was, somebody asked, "Are you sure you unwrapped everything?" Hmmm. I unscrewed the lid assembly and discovered a green seal blocking the filter. With that removed, water came through! Some things you just can't learn in a classroom.

It had stopped raining and warmed up, which brightened the mood of the whole camp. I cleaned the dead spiders out of my tent (a little less cowed by nature in the daylight) and made sure to zip the thing up more tightly than before to keep invaders out. It was never too early to gather firewood, so the men kept busy building an impressive pile of cut logs. Teli and I sawed together for a while, and he shared a bit more of his prepping philosophy. "The most important thing, obviously, is a phone," he said. He kept a solar-powered charging contraption in his bug-out bag and planned to download a lot of his basic personal information onto a small zip drive he could bring along if he had to bug out for real.

My primitive understanding of prepping was that it was strictly off the grid, as if preppers yearned to return to some kind of pre-industrial or biblical utopia. Yet an unstated theme of the whole event was that staying connected—that byword of harried, overprivileged, twenty-first-century narcissists—was one of the best things you could do to aid your survival. The experienced preppers all packed smartphones, radios, solar chargers, plenty of batteries and any other technology that might be helpful in a pinch. There was also a lot of planning about how to reach each other if chaos erupted and phones and email went down. (Mainly it requires two-way radios, repeaters and more know-how about electromagnetic signals than I'll probably ever have.)

I had felt vaguely like I was cheating while packing my bug-out bag with anything fancier than raw oatmeal, and in fact my girlfriend made fun of me when I came home from the store with some mini cheeses (fully wrapped in wax, so they keep well without refrigeration) and asked her to make sure nobody ate them since they were for the bug-out weekend. "I thought you were supposed to live off the land!" she hooted. "Okay, don't worry, I won't touch your 'survival' cheese. Want some survival Brie? How about I make you a little picnic basket?"

Maybe she was right, I thought. So I turned off my smartphone the moment I left my car at the bottom of the mountain and decided to get through the weekend without such modern privileges. Other preppers had their smartphones fully holstered, however, and nobody was shy about whipping out any comfort they brought from home. I even detected a bit of envy behind the disdain Jodi's gourmet *tonnino* elicited. The clincher came when Jason took a break from splitting wood and I heard him say, to nobody in particular, "Man, I know what I'm ordering when I get back: two cheeseburgers." Civilization envy, it turned out, was a normal part of prepping. That was all the signal I needed to turn my phone back on. To my surprise, I had service, so I sent text messages to a few pals, filling them in on the bug-out weekend so far.

The second night went much better than the first, with no burned clothing, dry tents for everybody and a much cheerier mood around the fire. I had loaded several books onto my iPad, which I didn't tell my girlfriend about but, if you think about it, makes perfect sense as a survival tactic because traditional books are heavy yet you can probably fit every survival manual ever written onto an iPad and bring them all with you, adding a mere pound and a half to your bug-out bag. I figured the *U.S. Army Survival Manual (FM 21–76)* might make good reading if there was down time on the excursion, so I pulled it up on my iPad and read a few choice excerpts to the group gathered round the fire. This passage, in particular, drew murmurs of recognition: "All of us were born kicking and fighting to live, but we have become used to the soft life. We have become creatures of comfort. We dislike inconveniences and discomforts. What happens when we are faced with a survival situation with its stresses, inconveniences, and discomforts? This is when the will to live—placing a high value on living—is vital."[2]

The will to sleep overcame the will to read aloud from the *Army Survival Manual,* so I turned in around, well, I have no idea what time it was, except it was dark and chilly, yet DRY! By comparison with the night before, it was like going from a drainage ditch to a bed at a Comfort Inn. Zipping my tent had been a miracle cure that kept the spiders out, and I have every reason to believe I slept by myself in there.

There was a surprise guest in the morning: Preston, who had seemed to be in fine spirits during the first night of the bug-out weekend (before it started to rain), but had then gone to bed and stayed in bed for the next 36 hours, sick with some kind of flu. Various members of the group had checked in on Preston from time to time to make sure he was still alive (which he was), yet his condition clearly made everybody wonder: What if that was me? When Preston finally rematerialized, he explained that his dinner on the first night had been a bag of Cuban black beans and rice he had purchased in bulk from a surplus store, then brought to life with boiling water heated on the fire. That must have been the culprit, he guessed—which seemed like quite a knee-slapper to Omar. "Cuban beans?" Omar cackled. "Who gets Castro's surplus food? Angola?" He had taken license with Preston's explanation, but that didn't prevent a lot of chuckling.

The weather was now mild again, almost as if that miserable rainy interlude had never happened. It was the last day of the bug-out excursion, and some of the preppers broke camp quickly. Jodi and Joe had packed up their spacious tent—a McMansion, compared with my little sliver of plastic—and checked out before some of the other preppers even emerged from their own tents. Others lingered. I was damn near enjoying myself as I whipped up another passable cup of coffee in my metal tin and sat contemplatively on a rock, enjoying actual warmth in my fingers, when I noticed that Jason seemed to be all business as he broke down his gear and started stuffing everything into his bag. Suddenly I felt a little panicky, like I might get left behind. So I, too, began to prepare for departure, except I had never repacked my tent before and had an awful time stuffing it into the sack, as everything that fit artfully into my bug-out bag when I had a week to prepare suddenly seemed to sprout appendages that exceeded the dimensions of my pack. It was shaping up as an anxious end to the whole experience until I heard Jason say, "Man, I can't wait to hit a bed." You and me both, brother.

My pack on the way down was a lot lumpier than it had been on the way up, but it didn't matter; I knew I no longer needed to find much of anything in there, and before long I'd just dump the whole jumble onto my bedroom floor at home anyway. As the last group of preppers sauntered down the mountain, I chatted for the first time with Arianna, an unmarried mom of two young kids with a master's degree in molecular biology who did medical research for a living. She had tried to build a family with her boyfriend, the father of her two kids, but both parents were miserable, so they arranged a more or less amicable split. I fished around for a wacky factor but didn't find one, and she seemed to be on the trip just to learn a bit of self-sufficiency so she'd be more comfortable if her life without a man persisted. "I always want to keep one eye open," she told me. "Now that I have kids, I feel I need to do that for them."

The plan, once we were down, was to hit a diner and treat ourselves to cooked food, which most of the group did, except for Jodi and Joe, who probably had organic lamb *au poivre* waiting in the crockpot at home. One by one, everybody hit the bathroom as discreetly as possible, to wash up and take advantage of the plumbing. We ate omelets and pancakes and burgers and had a few laughs about the PBS crew seeking out psychotics and the hipster preppers taking a walk on the wild side. Omar got the biggest laugh as he wondered out loud what ordinary people out for a brisk hike in the woods with their kids must have thought as they encountered a motley group of inner-city preppers led by a burly, tattooed and possibly murderous inner-city thug. "Whoa!" he imagined their reaction to be, as he unleashed a belly laugh. "Who's this black guy in the woods with an axe? Is there a cell signal up here? How do I reach 911?"

It's always great to get home after an uncomfortable trip, and after this one, I had no sentimental desire to return to Prepper Mountain. Yet I was surprised by the emotion I felt, which didn't come so much from shared misery, as happens sometimes, but from seeing the honest humanity of people I had underestimated at the beginning. I didn't accept everything the preppers seemed to stand for, but I did see in virtually all of them an earnest effort to confront things that worried and frightened them, to do something rather than nothing, to control what they could and curse what they couldn't. Benjamin Franklin and Henry Clay and Andrew Jackson would have approved, I think.

I concluded after the trip that I don't want to be a traditional prepper, at least not in a systematic, deliberate way. But it was also clear that the preppers I was with were a lot more self-sufficient than people who don't think much about what to do if the lights go off. Here are my four lessons from bugging out:

Prepping is a pain in the ass. The people who do it for real spend as much time and money on their avocation as people who are fanatics about tennis, fishing, stamp collecting or hitting the gym every day. There's no end of gear or new techniques, and you really do need to practice regularly in order to stay in top prepping shape. In this regard, the tyranny of prepping is the same as the tyranny of golf or shopping or fashion or collecting something, because once you get into it, you can become captive to the stuff somebody will always insist you must have or the new techniques you must learn. Go too far, and you end up sacrificing freedom rather than gaining it. I didn't enjoy prepping enough to turn it into a regular part of my life, and I'm not convinced the odds of a calamity are high enough to justify the investment.

Going it alone is a losing strategy. One common image of preppers is the Rambo-like lone survivor as the rest of humanity kills itself off. That might be plausible in the movies, but it's a silly idea in reality, and none of the preppers I met thought that way at all. Sure, you could learn the skills to survive on your own for weeks, months, maybe years. But withdrawing from society, or planning to, isn't freedom—it's a rejection of the freedoms society already offers. Sure, it would be great if we could take advantage of every resource society offers today while also preparing for the exhaustion of those resources. But those are two different mind-sets that don't usually exist in the same person. Lone survivalists withdraw even when they don't need to, something people do in psychological and emotional ways just as a woodsman might disappear into the wilderness. It might be liberating to know you can survive on your own if you have to, but it's also confining to live that way if you don't have to.

Community is salvation. Associating yourself with others you want to survive with is an essential element of self-reliance. Sure, there's merit to all the prepper gear and techniques, but the most powerful resource of all is other preppers. Jason didn't overtly teach us this insight, but it was a theme of the whole experience as strangers with a shared interest got to know and trust each other, share tips, stories and even food, and look out for each other. What we did on that weekend, whether knowingly or not, was build a community from scratch. It wasn't a lovefest and we didn't all part as bosom buddies, but we learned to rely on each other in ways that multiplied each person's individual resources.

Prepping light is the answer. It is for me, anyway. For most of the people in our group, Superstorm Sandy was a triggering event that revealed an uncomfortable lack of independence. It seemed we all knew the proverbial, clueless suburbanite who owned a generator that didn't work without the fuel he had forgotten to stockpile. So when the gas stations closed, their emergency preparations turned out to be useless. That's faux prepping—spending a few bucks on something trendy to make yourself feel rugged without bothering to invest in skills or knowledge that might be more valuable.

Teli, the New Jersey contractor, got it right when he wondered why anybody would decline to make a few modest preparations, just in case. A pragmatic, low-intensity emergency plan might include a good pair of waterproof boots (thoroughly broken in), a list of three or four friendly destinations you could easily reach on one tank of gas, a couple dozen Bic lighters, several pairs of gloves and, most important, a circle of people—friends, family members, neighbors and even occasional acquaintances—you can count on. And fill your car with gas before a storm!

NINE

THE CURSE OF COMFORT

THE PREPPERS I BUGGED OUT WITH WERE DEFINITELY not eager to go back in time and occupy some sort of nineteenth-century homestead. They enjoyed the privileges of living in or around New York City. They were prepping for disaster because they worried about something that might disrupt their way of life, not because they wanted to ditch their way of life. They'd only leave it behind if there were no other choice.

A lot of Americans, however, are seeking something akin to the physical frontier of the nineteenth century. There are off-the-gridders who aren't so impressed with our relentlessly networked society and check out, aiming for a simpler life purged of the cultural clutter that piles up around so many of us. Related to that are "permaculturists" who don't necessarily foreswear electricity and modern plumbing, but who want to disconnect from corporate assembly lines that pump an endless stream of products into our homes. Their goal is to grow as much of their own food as possible and perhaps grind their own toothpaste from mint and baking soda and make their own deodorant from coconut oil and arrowroot. A new "paleo" movement mimics the habits of early hunter-gatherers who lived on a diet of meat, meat, meat, nuts, a few legumes and more meat and didn't enjoy the benefits of orthotic shoe inserts or cucumber-infused moisturizing gel. Many others, not quite as dedicated, still want to do more for themselves while relying less on mass-produced wares. They express themselves by patronizing artisanal shopping sites such as Etsy, the DIY page on Pinterest and the maker site Quirky, and by seeking other forms of refuge from assembly-line sameness.

As with preppers, it's hard to count all the people who in one form or another seek some kind of escape from mainstream society. But it seems clear that something about the frontier still beckons, even if it's a subliminal calling. And the call has gotten louder as our economy has become more technocratic and the path to success has gotten rockier. When Frederick Jackson Turner wrote about the frontier in the 1890s, he said the western movement of Americans was a "return to primitive conditions. . . . This perennial rebirth, this fluidity of American life, this expansion westward with its new opportunities, its continuous touch with the simplicity of primitive society, furnish the forces dominating American character."[1] It's not hard to imagine many Americans today seeking some kind of rebirth or a place with new opportunities, even if they do so privately. More and more Americans feel they're not making it. They're stuck in the Liberty Trap and want out. They're eager to escape their mistakes or have more control over their destiny. If you feel overrun by new technology or other economic forces you don't fully understand, it might seem natural to seek routines you're more familiar with and rules that make it easier to win. A more "primitive society," as Turner referred to it, can be appealing when you feel disserved and exploited by the institutions that now dominate modern living.

For all its problems, however, institutional society also conveys many advantages we're not even aware of until they're gone. Nearly everybody wants to unplug and escape sometimes, and there's nothing new about wanting to jump off the hamster wheel—even permanently. But done too hastily or thoroughly, the quest for a fresh start can diminish economic freedom rather than enhance it. What might seem like a logical way to escape the Liberty Trap can drive you deeper into it. The trick is to maximize the advantages institutional society conveys while breaking free of its more confining elements. That requires more of a surgical withdrawal than outright flight, with the destination being more of a psychological frontier than a physical one.

Obviously there's no longer a western frontier in America, since the nation is settled all the way to the Pacific Ocean. Yet Turner's primitive society makes regular cameo appearances among people who can afford to break their routines for a little while and return to the mainstream whenever they wish. Sarah Palin has made a second career out of hunting caribou and exploring the Alaskan wilds (with a TV crew in tow), while fending off rumors that she spends more time at her estate in the resort community of Scottsdale, Arizona, than in her native Alaska.[2] For a year, the only meat Facebook founder Mark Zuckerberg would eat came from animals he had hunted or slaughtered himself, part of a new movement of locavores who aim to make more of a personal connection with the food they consume.[3] Harvard graduate John Durant, author of *The Paleo Manifesto*—one of perhaps 400 "paleo" titles available these days—got his start by hanging out in New York City with a group of "urban cavemen" who ate piles of organ meat followed by 24-hour fasts, and ran barefoot throughout the city for sport.[4]

Others seek a more literal frontier life amid still-wild pockets of the country. In the desert near Terlingua, Texas, about 15 miles from the Mexican border, Abe Connally and his wife, Josie, practice a kind of Internet homesteading. They live with their two boys in an adobe home they built with their own hands, relying on a homemade "energy infrastructure" and on water captured during infrequent rainstorms. They grow much of their own food and meat. "Because of our lifestyle, we don't have to earn as much," Abe Connally told a news reporter in an interview. "Instead of working 40-hour weeks for money, we work 5 to 10 hours a week." Unfortunately, some of their free time gets spent doing laundry on a washboard, the old-fashioned way, and doing a lot of other manual labor. Most off-the-gridders are untrackable—except, perhaps, by hound dog—since they cut ties to the Internet and the other networks we use to keep in touch these days. But the Connallys keep the world updated on their doings through their Web site, which features dozens of homesteading tips and proclaims the Connallys are "off grid and loving it," or on their Flickr page, which features thousands of family photographs showing the Connallys, well, off the grid and apparently loving it.[5]

Off-the-gridders typically live alone, in isolated settings or in Amish-style communities where they aren't dependent upon banks, food factories, TV networks, politicians, the Internet, power companies or magazines telling them how to dress and behave. There's obviously something appealing about ditching those institutionalized pressures. But it's a mistake to equate "primitive conditions" with simplicity. Primitive can actually be quite complicated. Division of labor is something most of us hardly ever think about because it's so integral to the way we live that flipping a light switch is something we're more inclined to notice. But step out of the modern economy for a moment and you'll immediately realize something is missing. Division of labor allows every individual worker to specialize in something and earn a living at it, rather than trying to manufacture everything he needs himself. The economy becomes far more efficient and workers earn a greater return on their human capital. Division of labor also allows one innovator to build on the work of another innovator, instead of everybody always starting from scratch. This has been one of humanity's most spectacular successes, allowing living standards to rise multifold generation after generation. It's responsible for virtually every medical advance, the great invention known as leisure time, and most of the things we enjoy, with the possible exception of sex. When you go back to living off the land, however, you sacrifice the profound advantages that come with division of labor. A certain type of freedom may come from raising your own chickens or digging your own latrine, but freedom is lost, too, when you reject modern efficiencies and do everything by hand. Is there really much joy to be had in cleaning your laundry on a washboard or hauling water around in buckets?

Digital connectivity is another oppressive marvel, either enriching your life or making it miserable—or both. One reason our temporal freedom—the wise use of time—is endangered is the explosion of things that demand our time. Many of those things are related to the social media networks we try to keep up with, the emails that never stop rolling in on our smartphones and the bosses and colleagues who now feel entitled to check in on us during evenings, weekends and other personal time that used to be sacrosanct. Cutting the cord is one way to reclaim your time, but that's a blunt instrument. Better to exploit the many ways connectivity itself can enhance our temporal freedom, through automated bill payment, online shopping, digital record-keeping and many other time-saving innovations. The art of living requires us to embrace technology that improves our fortunes while rejecting technology that doesn't, the real challenge being to figure out which is which. We've mythologized the frontier and focused on characteristics we consider positive, such as ruggedness and self-sufficiency. But we overlook the negative, such as the withdrawal from community and the flight from failure, when it might be more productive to confront failure and figure out what went wrong. "If you unplug too much you really do lose a lot of your freedoms," Arthur Bradley, the NASA engineer and prepper-guidebook author, told me. "Quality of life is not very good. Retreating to an underground shelter or something like that is probably not the best lifestyle."[6]

The real payoff comes from harnessing the grit, character and fresh opportunity a frontier experience can generate within the seams of the modern economy. A woman named Amy Savage, for instance, discovered the frontier in Washington, Pennsylvania, a notch on the old Rust Belt near the Appalachian Mountains in the southwestern part of the state near Ohio. In 2010, Savage was 28 and running a small, specialty trucking company with her boyfriend in Michigan.

That was a lousy time to be in Michigan. The auto industry was crawling back from a brutal recession that plunged two of the three domestic automakers into bankruptcy and caused thousands of lay-offs. Detroit, once a glorious American city, was about to stagger into bankruptcy itself. Savage's three flatbed trucks sat unused much of the time, her handful of employees idling along with them.

She read about the Marcellus Shale formation that ran through parts of New York, Pennsylvania, Ohio and West Virginia. New "hydrofracking" drilling techniques were suddenly allowing drillers to extract oil and gas from parts of the earth that had been inaccessible up till then. If she could relocate to someplace where drilling activity was picking up, she could use her trucks to move heavy oil and gas equipment. So she left her native Michigan and set up shop in a rural area that, until hydrofracking arrived, had been a fading steel and coal region. Once there, Savage changed her plan—something often necessary to capture opportunity, yet difficult for people uncomfortable with risk. While trying to buy fireproof sweatshirts for her crew, she realized there was no store anywhere nearby where workers could buy the kind of heavy-duty clothing they needed, at reasonable prices. So she used $50,000 of her savings to rent space, buy some inventory and open her own supply store. The customers came. So she opened another store, then a third, in different locations, expanding her offerings and service along the way. A few years after moving to the Marcellus Shale region, Savage's business employed several dozen people and was approaching $4 million in sales. A fresh start in the right place transformed stagnation into success.[7]

There are other frontier regions similar to the Marcellus that offer fresh opportunities for those willing to trek there. The Bakken Shale formation, concentrated mostly in North Dakota, has transformed a once nearly empty state into the world's newest energy hotbed. Some people go there for the lucrative hourly pay, which can easily be three or four times what they're able to earn wherever they came from. Others, like Savage, go to start businesses that benefit from the influx of people and all the money sloshing around. The need for workers is so urgent that the unemployment rate in North Dakota has fallen below 3 percent, which is about as low as it's possible to go, considering that some people are always unemployed because they're between jobs. In one sense this is a workers' paradise because virtually anybody capable of working can get a good-paying job. But like the old American frontier we have romanticized, it can be hard living. There's a shortage of housing, which pushes up rents and leaves some workers living in trailers or even cars. Men vastly outnumber women in this new oil country, a frustrating situation for members of both sexes. Locals complain that the energy boom has produced a corresponding surge in crime, drugs, noise, traffic and air pollution from the endless storm of tractor-trailers carrying supplies in and oil out. "This is like in the old days in the West, when the ghost towns were booming," says Jonnie Cassens, a California woman who went to North Dakota looking for a job during the 2008 recession and ended up working as a special-delivery truck driver. Life is better for her there than in California, but she laments the lack of a girlfriend or two to get her nails done with, and worries about the risk of living alone.[8]

Another frontier: America's "third coast," which hugs the Gulf of Mexico from the southern tip of Texas to the middle of western

Florida. This region is poised to thrive on account of increased trade with Latin America and greater energy production, just like North Dakota. The epicenter of this boom zone is Houston, which *Forbes* predicts will become "America's next great global city."[9] If the third coast is too muggy or buggy for you, there's other data showing which cities seem to offer the most overall opportunity these days. At the top of the list are San Jose and San Francisco (in other words, Silicon Valley) along with Washington, DC (the government will always fund itself), Seattle (Silicon Valley, with more earnestness) and Salt Lake City (as earnest as it gets). At the bottom: Charlotte, Milwaukee, Atlanta, Dayton and Indianapolis, which are fine cities, in their way, except they need to convince more businesses to show up and maybe woo the next Microsoft or Facebook.[10] And if big cities aren't your thing, consider farm country, which has been booming in many areas, benefiting from foreign demand for US crops and other factors.

Or we can look outside the United States to find American-style opportunity and the financial and economic freedom that comes with it. A number of other countries have better upward mobility than the United States, meaning there's a better chance of rising above the socioeconomic group you were born into. Research by economist Miles Corak identifies at least 14 foreign nations where it's easier to get ahead, including eight European countries, Canada, Australia, New Zealand, Singapore and even Pakistan. Go west, young man? Maybe you should go to South Asia instead. Or to China, which is growing in impressive spurts much as the adolescent America of the 1800s did (with a communist government thrown in as an extra challenge). A New Zealand woman named Natalie Sisson says she finds "freedom in business and adventure in life" by living in many of those places, and more. The "suitcase entrepreneur," as she fashions herself, has no permanent residence and moves constantly from country to country, living with friends and locals whenever possible. She earns a living from blogging, writing, speaking and coaching others how to be a "digital nomad" able to run a business from anywhere.[11]

Some hearty folks find their way to these frontier regions and profit from the journey. But for many of us the real frontier is a new attitude or mind-set rather than a place. "The frontiers of our economic system are formed by our mental attitude and our unity," Harold Stassen, governor of Minnesota and frequent presidential candidate, said all the way back in 1946.[12] It's still true, perhaps even more so now that our civic institutions have become less effective. Historian Neil Howe thinks ruggedness—the chief attribute of a frontiersman, whether mythologized or real—is something better thought of today as mental toughness than as physical domination of nature. "I don't think we mean literally physically rugged anymore," he says. "I think we mean rugged as a psychological trait, a temperament, an ability to handle stuff."[13] The frontier of the 1800s required considerable physical and mental toughness. The attitudinal frontier of the twenty-first century is an easier place to survive since you don't have to hunt your own food, harvest wood for heat or create your own entertainment.

Yet even this psychological frontier can be a daunting place, with many people lacking the grit and the willingness to take risks that are often prerequisites of success. For one thing, fewer Americans move from place to place than at any time since the end of World War II. Internal migration, as it is known, has been a major strength of the US economy for decades, as people who can't find enough opportunity in one place look for it someplace else. In a way, the whole history of

America is basically the story of people moving around to make better lives for themselves. That's why Europeans came to America in the first place. It's why wagon trains moved west in the 1800s, why rural citizens moved to cities in the early 1900s, why northerners in decaying Rust Belt cities moved south in recent decades. But our movement as a nation is slowing, like an oldster who's not as spry as he used to be.

The proportion of Americans moving in a given year hit a record low recently and is barely half what it was in the 1950s.[14] The housing bust that began in 2006 has something to do with it, since millions of homeowners got stuck with negative equity in their homes and would lose money if they had to move—a powerful incentive for staying put. But something else seems to be going on. Of the people who do move around, they're more likely to move someplace where housing and living costs are lower than to move somewhere with low unemployment and ample opportunity—as if desperately chasing living standards that are slipping away. In the Marcellus Shale region Amy Savage moved to, there's so much demand for welders and other skilled tradespeople that they can earn $150,000 per year or more—pay that most college graduates would jump at.[15] Yet there's a shortage of welders there. The training must be too tough, or it must be too strenuous to move where the jobs are. By most measures, Americans are clinging to comfort instead of taking risks and striving for something better.

Some analysts call this fragile group of head-hangers the "precariat," a phrase first used in Europe to describe people with precarious living standards, dim prospects and little confidence in themselves or the society they live in.[16] The American precariat includes a lot of people who crave the fresh start a frontier experience offers, yet fear the primitive conditions it might entail. So they cling to comfort as freedom slips away. And soon the comfort begins to slip away, too.

Crawling out of the Liberty Trap entails risk, the same way escaping from any punishing situation entails risk. You might go a direction that makes you even worse off instead of leading to freedom. Yet it's obviously risky to stay in the Liberty Trap and do nothing, because your financial freedom will continually erode and leave you leading some life other than the one you want. Americans admire the rugged individual who's willing to take risk and dust himself off after a fall. They imagine themselves to be like that. But many are not. During the last 80 years, American society has evolved from the "Greatest Generation" that survived the Depression and won World War II into an even more privileged society that some experts believe is drowning in narcissism. Self-reliance has become self-gratification. "There's an emphasis on uniqueness and greatness, and things being personalized for the individual," says psychologist Jean Twenge, coauthor of *The Narcissism Epidemic*. "But it's not about being independent and standing on your own two feet."[17] Much individualism today is characterized by "mass customization"—being able to order any color combo as long as it can be programmed into the assembly line, which, increasingly, it can. The veneration of the self is a focal cultural activity—through social-media updates, overparenting and, of course, selfies. Apple CEO Steve Jobs must have known what he was doing when he named the iPod, iPhone and iPad, because nothing appeals to American consumers more than something that starts with *I*.

So what should we do about an economy that requires more willingness to take risks by people who are afraid to leave the house? As usual, the wonks in Washington have plenty of policy ideas, such as government-subsidized "moving vouchers" that would help create more mobility and other ways to create an "opportunity society."[18] Or instead of relying on government solutions that will probably never materialize, we could forget about Washington and look for other ways to harness the timeless characteristics of frontier living, such as the practical, inventive turn of mind, the masterful grasp of material things, the restless, nervous energy and the dominant individualism that Frederick Jackson Turner described more than a century ago.[19] In simpler terms, we can perhaps characterize all of that as grit, ingenuity and ambition.

To survive on the frontier, the homesteaders of yore had to be continually vigilant—of weather, wildlife, their fellow humans and all other sorts of risks and dangers. We ought to heed their example, by being far more alert to what is changing, preparing for it, remaining ready for opportunity and never getting too comfortable. It sounds a lot easier than it is because society today places a premium on comfort, which is the enemy of opportunity. Comfort for the masses may be the signature accomplishment of Western culture since the end of World War II. Nearly everybody these days has a phone, TV, access to laundry machines, decent bedding, plenty of fast food and an Internet connection—even the poor. Yet comfort is also the bait inside the Liberty Trap. It lures us into inaction, like an opiate. It deadens the impulse to seek opportunity, to get out of Dodge, to explore, to inquire, to invent. Comfort is the biggest difference between dissatisfied people today and 100 years ago—we have it; they didn't. When you're dissatisfied but comfortable, it's easy to complain and do nothing. But when you lack even the most basic comforts, such as food, shoes or heat in the winter, the frontier, wherever or whatever it is, seems a lot more inviting. Many of the early pioneers we admire set out for the frontier because they had no choice. The privation they endured while living off the land would probably kill most of us today, but for them, it was better than staying put. Most of us have far better choices now, because we can do nothing and still enjoy basic comforts. Yet there we are in the Liberty Trap, comfortable enough to stay put and gaze at the frontier through binoculars. Today's frontier—whether an energy-rich badland populated by roughnecks, an undiscovered digital domain or a new way of thinking about the same old challenges—does offer the promise we rightly associate with undiscovered territory. There are still places you can go and things you can do to get a fresh start. It's not the frontier that has gone missing, but rather the frontier mentality—the inventive turn of mind, the grasp of material things, the continuous touch with simplicity. We rail against establishment conformity and the evils of government and corporate institutions, yet we tacitly embrace those same institutions for the comforts they convey. The Liberty Trap is nicely appointed and climate-controlled. That's why it doesn't seem like a trap.

TEN

AMERICAN DREAM
INFLATION

THE FIRST TIME I BOUGHT A HOME, IN THE 1990S, everybody offered this advice: stretch. Buy as much real estate as you can afford, and then some. You'll grow into it. Money will come. In a few years, you'll be sorry you didn't buy more.

That was a reasonable way to think about buying a home from 1950 to 2000 or so, but it would come off as terrible advice today. Millions of people who "stretched" to buy a home during the last 10 or 15 years ended up deeply regretful: either underwater on homes that plunged in value and were suddenly worth less than the buyers paid, or so behind on mortgage payments that they may as well have just signed the foreclosure papers when they closed on the property. The story of the subprime crisis and the housing bust that began around 2006 is familiar by this point, yet we still haven't fully adjusted to the ways it changed the quest for the American Dream and the financial freedom the Dream represents.

Historian James Truslow Adams coined the phrase "American Dream" in 1933 in a book called *The Epic of America*. He didn't stipulate owning a home or any of the other materialistic pleasures we have come to associate with the American Dream. Here's how Adams defined it: "That dream of a land in which life should be better and richer and fuller for everyone, with opportunity for each according to ability or achievement. . . . It is not a dream of motor cars and high wages merely, but a dream of social order in which each man and each woman shall be able to attain to the fullest stature of which they are innately capable, and be recognized by others for what they are, regardless of the fortuitous circumstances of birth or position."[1] The American Dream, in short, was the freedom to make the most you could out of yourself. Since Adams wrote in the early days of the Depression—when regular meals were a luxury to many—the society he described may have literally seemed like a dream out of most people's reach.

Today, by contrast, we tend to regard the American Dream as something we're entitled to as a birthright and something that should alarm us if it's unavailable. In 1933, when Adams published his book, only about 45 percent of adult Americans owned the homes they lived in, according to Census Bureau data, and the homeownership rate was going down, not up, on account of the Depression.[2] Owning a home was challenging even before then, because banks were disinclined to lend large sums to ordinary people, and when they did, they typically demanded a down payment of 30 to 40 percent, which many were unable to muster. But dream inflation has brought the idea of owning a home from the fringes of the American Dream to the center. A number of changes over time made owning a home cheaper and easier, including government programs that effectively subsidized homeownership for almost everybody who buys one. Consumer debt also became far more common starting around the late 1970s, partly because of innovations in finance and partly because the stigma of debt—ruinous to millions during the Depression—began to wear off as new generations saw how borrowing could boost their living standards. Billionaire financier George Soros would later call this a "superbubble" in which a growing mountain of debt created the illusion of prosperity.[3] But for the time being, the monthly-payment mentality—taking on as much debt as your income could cover each month—seemed to work. Lending standards eased and required down payments fell to as low as 3 percent under some government-backed loans—and even 0 percent, if you could find an adventurous bank. The American Dream morphed into a contractual agreement known as a 30-year mortgage. The homeownership rate, which was 44 percent in 1940, rose sharply after World War II and hovered between 63 and 65 percent for most of the 1960s, 1970s, 1980s and 1990s. It broke out of that range in 1997 and peaked at 69 percent in 2005, as reckless lending and other factors fueled a housing bubble bound to burst. The housing bust that followed brought the homeownership rate back to about 65 percent, which many economists consider a rough historical norm.[4]

So in a way we're back where we were 20 years ago, except there have been approximately 49,317,482 media reports during the last few years lamenting the "death of the American Dream." The question is: *Which* American Dream? The fabricated one politicians talk about on the campaign trail, when they insist voters have an inalienable right to easy living? The heavily financed one in which you can have almost anything you want?* The one you see in ads and commercials, in which smiling people live bountiful, effortless lives that you can, too, if only you call 1–800-BUY-THIS? Or something closer to the one Adams talked about 80 years ago, where there's opportunity to get ahead but no guarantees? If you believe the American Dream involves the traditional sequence of ever-larger homes, paid for with borrowed money backed by a stable career in which promotions come every three years on schedule, then it probably is dead. But if you take the home and the stability out of it, America is still a good place to seek opportunity according to ability or achievement.

Here's what has changed, without much notice: Owning a home, for many people, has actually become an impediment to achieving the American Dream. Making a long-term commitment to live in one place can sharply inhibit financial freedom these days because we live in a fast-changing economy with shifting prosperity zones. Among homeowners, the internal mobility rate—the percentage of people who move every year—is only about 4.5 percent. Among renters, it's more than six times as high—about 29 percent. Homeowners end up stuck in place because of "lock-in effects" that include stagnant or falling home values and incomes, few opportunities to get a better job that pays more and tighter credit standards than in the past, which make it harder to purchase another home.[5] Staying put wouldn't be such a big deal in a predictable and growing economy in which living

---

*Transaction charges, penalty fees and usurious interest rates may apply.

standards steadily improved. But that's not the economy that exists in many places. Instead, the familiar twin disruptors of globalization and the digital revolution are rapidly eviscerating segments of the economy that can't keep up, while strengthening other sectors that happen to thrive amid automation and offshoring. If you give up the flexibility to go where opportunity is—as many Americans have, most of them unwittingly—you've merged into the socioeconomic slow lane, which leads straight into the Liberty Trap. Maybe that's part of the reason that between 25 and 50 percent of people who buy a home end up saying they regret the decision.[6]

My own industry, journalism, is a good example of the American Dream morphing into a trap. Not long ago, you could be a national news correspondent while living in one of at least a dozen US cities, including Atlanta, Miami, New Orleans, Dallas, Chicago, Denver and Seattle. The advent of the Internet transformed the entire industry, causing plunging revenue, aggressive consolidation and the demise of long-standing print periodicals such as *U.S. News & World Report* (which I used to work for), *Newsweek* and *Ladies' Home Journal.* The venerable *Reader's Digest* declared bankruptcy twice, four years apart. At news organizations that survived, the economics of a revamped business model no longer left room for full-time correspondents earning decent salaries in cities other than New York, Washington, DC, San Francisco and perhaps Los Angeles, the epicenter of celebrity misbehavior and, therefore, ratings. So if you had built a career in journalism and put down roots somewhere in the heartland, you could move to one of a handful of high-cost coastal cities and compete with everybody else doing the same thing, or find another line of work. Either way, owning a home and committing to

fixed mortgage payments probably complicated the decision; it presented a big barrier to moving and a high financial bar to meet if you
stayed to start in some new field, probably near the bottom of the
income ladder. I know several people who faced this sort of dilemma.
Mostly they worked it out: by relying more on a spouse for a second
income, changing careers or downsizing their lifestyles. But it was
more like going backward than forward and not the kind of progress
somebody expects to make in the middle of a career.

Similar strains have occurred in many industries during the last
decade or so, ranging from blue-collar fields such as construction and
manufacturing to white-collar ones such as architecture, finance and
law. There's a general impression that the wealthy are living blissfully
these days, with only middle- or lower-income Americans struggling.
But many among the rich have gotten trapped by debt and blithe
expectations about their ability to "stretch," just as millions of others
have. From 2011 to 2014, for example, there were more than 70,000
foreclosures nationwide on homes valued at more than $500,000.
That's a lot of people who seemed wealthier than they were and
probably considered themselves to be so, too, which is why they got
into trouble.[7] Celebrity photographer Annie Leibovitz, who report-
edly earned as much as $250,000 per day for some photo shoots, fell
millions of dollars behind on debt she owed in the late 2000s and re-
sorted to forced sales of much of her portfolio to appease her lenders.[8]
One of those lenders was a company called Art Capital Group, which
specializes in loans to well-heeled artists and their patrons and often receives masterworks pledged as collateral when presumably rich
borrowers basically default on their loans.[9] Technology entrepreneur
Halsey Minor, who helped launch well-known businesses such as

CNET, Salesforce and Rhapsody, declared bankruptcy in 2013 after blowing a fortune estimated as large as $300 million on bad art and real estate deals.[10] A Manhattan glamour couple, Kent and Elizabeth Swig—both inheritors of real estate fortunes—endured an epic downfall and divorce after the 2008 collapse of Lehman Brothers and the implosion of the commercial debt market wrecked a property empire worth as much as $3 billion.[11] Their marriage, once regarded as a merger of real estate baronies, ended as a litigious war between the two families. Then there are the dozens of easy-come-easy-go celebrities who waste a fortune and then wail about how tough their lives are.

There's a common thread connecting glamourpusses forced to auction art and everyfolk struggling to put food on the table: New rules determine success these days, but they've never been published and most people don't know what they are. Meanwhile, most people—from hopeful high school students to corporate executives and even Wall Street traders—are abiding by old rules that may have been valid in the 1980s or 1990s but are now obsolete. Here are three Old Rules of Success that are driving people into the Liberty Trap, and three New Rules that will steer you away from the Liberty Trap:

Old Rule: If you work hard and get a good education, you'll get ahead. If only! These might be prerequisites of success, but it's wishful thinking to expect that if you "play by the rules," society will reward you. Society doesn't care whether you succeed or not, or how hard you work. And too many people these days work hard at something nobody's willing to pay money for. Our national leaders would be doing everybody a favor if they stopped perpetuating the outdated idea that getting an education—in anything—and working hard—at anything—are enough to succeed. What they fail to mention is there's this thing called a market out there, and if the market isn't willing to pay much for what you've got—whether you're offering trinkets, education or a particular skill set—then face facts: It's not worth much.

New Rule: If you want to earn a living, figure out what somebody is willing to pay you for. Forget about your passion, your dreams and what you feel you deserve. Be a ruthless capitalist and figure out how to meet an unmet need—and work hard at that. When demand dries up, find another unmet need, and so on, and adapt ad nauseam until you've banked so much money you can enjoy a true luxury: no longer having to adapt. Education almost always helps, but not at any cost. So do your best to invest shrewdly in education—for your whole life—and insist on a strong return on that investment. "The world is full of educated derelicts," Calvin Coolidge famously said. These days, educated derelicts are often poor as well.

Old Rule: Anybody can succeed in America. Technically, it's true. In reality, however, the odds of being successful as an adult have gotten higher for people born into high-income families and lower for people born into low-income families. It's still possible for people to rise from the gutter, the way we imagine success to happen in America. But two babies, one born into a family in the twentieth income percentile and one born into the eightieth, could have nearly identical innate abilities but vastly different opportunities available to them, leading one to become a model citizen and the other to become an economic dropout.[12]

New Rule: Surrounding yourself with elites pays off. This may be an odious development that augurs societal rot. But it doesn't change the fact that your odds of succeeding are better if you find a way to join the fraternity of haves—people able to help open doors your whole life—than if you plant yourself defiantly outside the gate.[13] It would be better for everybody—elites included—if class barriers were getting lower rather than higher. But nobody, not even determined national leaders, can do much about societal shifts that are beyond the reach of most laws or policies. The earlier in life you (or your kids) can climb the wall into the next socioeconomic stratum, and the one after that, the better off you'll be.[14] One of the best ways parents can do this is to scrimp, save and even cheat if necessary to get their kids into the best school district they can—and endure the putdowns of snooty gatekeeper parents who might resent the interloping.

Old Rule: Financial freedom requires stability. In macroeconomic terms this is true, since it's easier to get ahead in a nation with a stable government and a steady economy than in one characterized by turmoil. But at a personal level, stability and its cousins—safety, security and comfort—can generate complacency and decay. In *Antifragile: Things That Gain from Disorder*, risk expert Nassim Nicholas Taleb argues that organisms thrive when forced to adapt to volatility, but stagnate and atrophy when stress is absent. "We have been fragilizing the economy, our health, political life, education, almost everything . . . by suppressing randomness and volatility," he says.[15] This is how comfort lures us into the Liberty Trap: It signals progress and represents a reward for success, yet it's also an opiate that suppresses ambition and survival instincts that are important when something goes wrong.

New Rule: Financial freedom requires mobility. When prosperity was widespread and much of the wealth created in America stayed in America, you could stay in one place a long time, maybe your whole life, and enjoy plenty of opportunity to get ahead. But that hasn't always been the case, and for the time being it seems wise for ambitious strivers to be prepared to hunt for opportunity because the nation's prosperity zones are moving targets. If you're a fisherman and the shoreline shifts, you don't stand where the water used to be, waiting for it to return. You go where the fish are or you have a pretty boring day.

This might all sound pretty gloomy—if you consider yourself hopelessly mediocre and captive to trends beyond your control. Thankfully, there are still plenty of Americans who can't stand the thought of themselves as mediocre and will do whatever they can to gain an edge. Young Americans—the supposedly narcissistic, selfie generation known as the millennials—are so far showing less interest in committing to big purchases like cars and homes than their parents did. This is an alarming development to automakers, home builders and many others who rely on maxed-out consumer spending to remain profitable. But the millennials could be on to something. It could be they're taking all the big steps in life—starting a career,

getting married, buying cars and homes—later than their parents did simply because they lack the money. Even if that's the case, such forced frugality could end up enhancing their financial freedom by allowing them more flexibility and mobility than people who lock themselves into major life commitments. Besides, the many unhappy examples of people graduating from college with student-loan debt equivalent to Estonia's GDP and job prospects limited to barista or blogger might just instill a lasting dedication to thrift. These are people coming of age at a time when self-righteous Wall Streeters and mendacious politicians make the world seem broken. To them, the individualism of the baby boomers connotes greed and cynicism. Teamwork and communalism seem better.

There's actually plenty of room for Americans to tighten their belts without feeling a great deal of stress. Consider housing. In 1973, the average size of a new home was 1,660 square feet, and three people lived in the average home. That's an average of about 550 square feet of living space per person. Today, the average new home is nearly 2,600 square feet, and only 2.6 people live in the average home. That's about 990 square feet of living space per person, or an 80 percent increase during the last 40 years. Some of that represents a genuine improvement in living standards. When I moved from a three-bedroom house with one bathroom to a larger home with three bathrooms—and no longer had to battle my two teenage kids for the shower—it definitely made my life better. But there's also a point of diminishing returns at which extra space doesn't really buy us extra freedom of any kind. We're just spending extra for it because . . . well, why are we? The big things we spend money on are generally nice to have, but if you had to sign a contract when you committed to them, agreeing to give up economic freedom in exchange for a wine cellar, his and her bathrooms and a home theater, would you?

We also tend to consider it a kind of failure if more than one generation of adults ever has to live in the same house together. If kids move back in with their parents after college, it's mortifying for the kids and aggravating for the parents, who can never seem to truly empty the nest. Our elderly parents only live with us in their dotage if there's not enough money for the Sunrise Club or whatever the local retirement home is called. Yet one of the supposed strengths of Old America—the one we romanticize as more pure and authentic than the New, Profane America we live in—was family cohesion. Parents and grandparents and sons and daughters and brothers and sisters took care of each other, whether it meant sharing a home, lending money when necessary, putting them to work in the family business or supporting them when they couldn't support themselves. As with much of American history, some mythology fuels that ideal; Americans have traditionally been leavers who are quite willing to kiss Mom goodbye if there's a better deal down the river or on the other side of the mountain. Still, our ancestors would think us ninnies for calling it a "crisis" when families have to double up and share a bedroom or take turns in the shower.

Then there's stuff. Goods. Consumerism. Here are a few enlightening facts about people who qualify as poor today, according to federal poverty thresholds: The average amount of living space per person among people below the poverty line is 515 square feet, roughly the same as for the entire country 40 years ago—and more than the average household in Europe today. Virtually every household qualifying as poor has a refrigerator, stove, oven and color TV; 80 percent have air conditioning and 75 percent own at least one automobile, according to research by California entrepreneur Kip Hagopian and UCLA economist Lee Ohanian.[16] Conservative commentators often cite such statistics to argue that the poor have it pretty good and ought to stop asking for handouts. There's another way to look at it. If the poor have that much, how much do the rest of us have? It's pretty easy to conclude: We have way more than we need. Way, way more.

I could rant about the gaudy homes, cars and boats of the 1 percent, and their robber-baron lifestyles, but that would be tiresome. Instead of picking on the rich—who are already burdened with too much unjust criticism; just ask them—I'll pick on myself. I'm pretty flinty, with an instinctive fear of coming up short that probably stems from a divorce that left me underfinanced for several years. So when I moved recently and had to pack up closets and basement storage nooks and all the odds and ends laying around, I was appalled to discover how much unnecessary stuff I had. The worst of it was stuff I had bought for my two kids as birthday or holiday gifts that had gone totally unused. There were clothes with tags still on them and toys that seemed to have gotten shoved into a closet right out of the box. My kids had also built an impressive collection of wasted gift cards, which were purchased by me or various relatives and then promptly misplaced. Gift cards are aptly named but for reasons other than we believe; they are actually a gift to the merchant rather than the customer because somebody spent $25 or $50 that in many cases will never be redeemed. Then there was my own stuff: sweaters and kitchen gadgets and lawn paraphernalia and fantasy sports gear I must have purchased while under the influence of prescription pharmaceuticals, because I had no recollection of ever buying it or using it.

I pride myself on being able to resist impulse buys and go without things I'd really like to have. But I had to admit I was fooling myself. (Again!) I had become an overspender, driven by two powerful phenomena. One was the forced buying I engaged in because I felt obligated to. The biggest forced splurge came every year at Christmas, when I spent hundreds of dollars on gifts for my kids that served no purpose except to perpetuate a multigenerational consumerist orgy. Most parents who celebrate Christmas know the awful sensation of shopping for gifts for your kids: You start by picking up a few things you're excited to give them, then you wonder if that's enough and before you know it you've blown your whole budget until the following summer. The kids tear through their gifts like they're on a sugar binge, then an hour later are totally bored. You vow to make a better impression the following Christmas, when you buy even more stuff. This is how we've turned a religious holiday into a march of zombie shoppers moaning "buy, buy, buy." Other types of forced buying occur because the nearly $200 billion worth of ads and commercials flashed before our faces every year actually work. Like many other people, I like to consider myself ad-proof, impervious to anybody's efforts to tell me how to spend my money. Ha. Advertising is so powerful and effective that we actually buy far larger homes these days so we have space to store all the stuff we'll inevitably buy. Closets barely existed in the homes of 100 years ago. Today there are closets bigger than the bedrooms our grandparents slept in.[17]

The second phenomenon compelling me to spend way more than necessary is credit. Nearly every retail purchase I make goes on a credit card, which makes shopping more pleasant. When I pay for something in cash, it gives me a queasy feeling—an actual sense of loss. So I pay by credit to avoid feeling bad. Clearly I'm not alone in this. There's nothing new about the idea of credit, which goes back centuries, but the use of credit to buy anything and everything is a modern development that has transformed personal finance. The Federal Reserve didn't start tracking credit card debt until 1968, when Americans racked up a meager $2 billion in purchases on plastic. That has soared to about $900 billion today, a 450-fold increase.[18] The overall economy, meanwhile, grew by a mere 18-fold during the same time span.[19] Credit cards have become so common that in a nation of nearly 320 million people (including children) there are 400 million credit card accounts.[20] The rate of personal bankruptcies has risen in tandem with the explosion of credit, and more people would be bankrupt if interest rates hadn't been near record lows for the last several years.[21] Credit certainly has its place in a healthy economy, but it has become so unconstrained that it's now a huge liability for millions of Americans—and a sneaky invitation into the Liberty Trap.

Off-the-gridders tend to reject consumerist culture in its entirety. But you don't have to go that far. Better to assess which elements of modern culture constrain your financial freedom and which enhance it, and carefully pull the weeds while cultivating the flowers. A loose movement of anticonsumerist purists known as "minimalists," "essentialists," "life hackers" or "declutterers" are doing just that. The goal is to live contentedly on necessities and a few extras that genuinely make life better, while shunning many other modern contrivances. And this you can do while staying plugged into mainstream culture. A guy named Joshua Fields Millburn, for instance, got off to a roaring start in his career, earning a six-figure salary with Cincinnati Bell, but he then quit at the age of 30 after his mother died at the same time he was getting divorced. Something about working nights and weekends to earn a lot of money, and still ending up $100,000 in debt, seemed unfulfilling, so he sold most of his stuff, declared a moratorium on shopping, severely downsized, lost 80 pounds and paid off his debts. A friend, Ryan Nicodemus, noticed that the dour Millburn had suddenly cheered up and, after learning why, decided to join him in launching a Web site devoted to a minimalist lifestyle and writing a book called *Everything that Remains*. "Happiness," they write, "is a life that is filled with passion and freedom, a life in which we grow as individuals and contribute beyond ourselves. Growth and contribution: those are the bedrocks of happiness. Not stuff." They now go around the country lecturing about how to simplify your life without giving up TV, email or your job.[22]

Minimalists enhance their financial and economic freedom by reducing or eliminating their dependence on things without necessarily sacrificing the virtuous aspects of modernity. They focus on pragmatic steps rather than dramatic lifestyle changes. One tactic is to have a large portion of your income automatically deposited into a savings account, not to be touched, while living off the paltry remainder. On average, Americans now save about 5 percent of their disposable income, which is something to be proud of given that the savings rate was barely 2 percent as recently as 2005.[23] But financial professionals advise us to save at least 10 percent of our income, and there's nothing wrong with saving 30 or 70 or 90 percent, if you can get by on the rest. It's almost un-American to save so much and spend so little, but the Federal Reserve would probably come up with some kind of bailout plan in the unlikely event that Americans stopped shopping. At any rate, nobody should ever feel guilty about saving too much.

Another minimalist tactic is to get rid of one item a day for as long as you can (without replacing the discarded stuff with new stuff). Recruit a friend or two and create a kind of buddy system so somebody is there to talk you down if you suddenly feel the urge to upgrade your smartphone or doorbust at Walmart on Thanksgiving. Turn off the digital screens as often as you can and interact more with people. And here's a big suggestion from Millburn and Nicodemus: Sell your home, if you own one, and rent instead, so you'll have more flexibility and freedom. That's not a flaky idea. In some of the world's most stable economies, such as Germany and Switzerland, the homeownership rate is far lower than it is in United States. Nations with high homeownership rates, by contrast, include Greece, Romania and other places with living standards nobody envies.[24] If you're not in a position to sell your home, Millburn and Nicodemus advise, then rearrange other parts of your life, by paying down debts, digitizing paperwork and shedding unneeded possessions so you'll be better prepared to sell if you have to. "It's just a bunch of wood and stone and wires," the two minimalists advise. "It should not be a fixture that defines you."[25]

Greg McKeown, a Stanford University lecturer and author of a book called *Essentialism*, points out that when the word *priority* came into the English language in the 1400s, it meant one, single important thing, and there was only a singular form. It stayed that way for 500 years. Turning *priority* into *priorities* was a twentieth-century innovation, yet if we return to the original meaning of the word, there can't really be many important single things. There can only be one. McKeown advises dedicating a few minutes each week to determining what that week's single priority is going to be, while at the same time committing to all the things you are not going to do, no matter how much others insist you should. A key test of your commitment to true essentialism, he says, is your ability to say no not just to frivolous activities but also to things that are important—in order to devote yourself to something that's even more important. Better to do one thing extremely well than do many things just well enough to scrape by.[26]

I've vowed more than once to adopt minimalist strategies and essentialize my life. Yet the stuff keeps coming and the priorities continue to mount. Part of the reason is teenage kids, who are venturing deeper into the consumerist maze and its endless corridors of clothing, gadgets and digitalia at the same time I'm trying to find my way out. But there's one other reason I remain more of a maximalist than a minimalist: After a dozen years as a renter, I bought a home again. That transformed me from a saver into a one-man economic stimulus program since I committed myself not just to mortgage payments but to new appliances, tools, contractors, lawn equipment and continual home improvements. This was the second house I had bought, and this time nobody urged me to "stretch." Instead, they urged me to stay well within my means, make sure I had a sizable cash cushion in case something went wrong, and plan to live in the house for a long time if I wanted the "investment" to pay off.

I don't mind any of that. I realize now that the American Dream requires sacrifices and trade-offs, and even then it might not pan out. There are other things I'd like to have but can't spend money on, because the mortgage comes first. So as the minimalists advise, I need to pare my life in other ways to make owning a home less confining. I also placed a bet on the area where I live, near New York City, which is one of many places in America that's directly plugged into the global economy. That enhances economic opportunity and adds resilience. And to some extent I gambled that America as a whole will emerge from its funk, build wealth again and reward ordinary people who take risks and invest in the future. I might not win that bet. But I'm glad I placed it.

ELEVEN

A LITTLE LEARNING IS STILL
A DANGEROUS THING

IMAGINE LIVING IN A COUNTRY IN WHICH THE GOV-
ernment decides who lives or dies, cars randomly explode at gas stations, more people receive welfare checks than paychecks and people
go around marrying horses.

Sounds like some banana republic, or maybe Caligula's Rome,
but this is actually America today—if you're gullible enough to believe what you hear. These are a few of the more colorful myths that
have circulated widely—mostly because of the Internet—and duped a
surprising number of people into believing outlandish nonsense. The
secret to this con game is that people tend to believe things they want
to be true, even, sometimes, when they're fantastical. When a crazy
rumor "confirms" some suspicion about a hated politician, a threatening class of people or some mysterious technology, it provides a way

out: it's easier to believe external forces are causing nettlesome problems than to finger ourselves as the cause. But when you look outward for the cause of problems that originate inward, you're forfeiting the freedom that comes from fixing the problem.

Here are the facts behind those lies I just ticked off. First are the notorious "death panels" that are supposedly part of government health-care reform—secret star chambers composed of faceless bureaucrats who decide which patients qualify for life-saving medical treatment and which die in the gutter as doctors and nurses step over them, powerless to help. This old lie has been thoroughly debunked, yet determined conspiracy theorists simply group the debunkers with the death panelists as part of the conspiracy. It is true that insurance companies used to make life-or-death decisions along these lines when they denied coverage for certain illnesses to customers who didn't meet the right criteria. That still happens today, though new laws make it less likely. And we can't spend endless amounts on costly care that could keep people alive for only a few additional days or weeks. But if the government is killing anybody, it's through bureaucratic ineptitude or do-nothing neglect. Anybody who chooses to believe government death panels are playing the Grim Reaper pretty much needs a reason to explain why everything seems to be beyond their control. Supervillains—riiiiiight.[1]

Automobiles blow up occasionally at gas stations because of cell phones. You're following that, right? Oh, sorry. See, here's what happens: When the cell phone rings, it creates a tiny spark, which ignites the gasoline fumes that have somehow escaped that gizmo on the end of the gas pump designed specifically to trap fumes, and escaped in such massive quantities that the poor bastard pumping gas with his cell phone in one hand is obliterated in a gigantic explosion. If you happened to get one of the emails—"WARNING FROM THE SHELL OIL COMPANY"—describing this dangerous situation, you know that cell phones must never be used near filling stations, lawnmowers, boats, etc., and if you've actually done this hundreds of times in your life and never been blown up, and so has everybody you know and they've never been blown up either, well, it can only be because . . . Wait! You're thinking too hard. Just forward this email to everybody you know and spread the fear.[2]

One chain email many people have seen claims, alarmingly, that in 11 states there are more people drawing welfare benefits paid for by taxpayers than there are taxpayers paying the benefits, which tells you everything you need to know about who's really ruining this country—people who are terrible at math. It's true there are a lot of people dependent on benefits or handouts from a taxpayer-funded government that won't be able to afford such largesse in the future. Here's how to make that problem sound 10 times worse: Count every Social Security and Medicare recipient, teacher, soldier, cop, firefighter and government worker as a welfare recipient, because their livelihoods come, in one form or another, from taxpayer funds. Never mind that most of those people work or used to work at regular jobs, have contributed to the economy and have never drawn anything resembling welfare. Skipping a few details and applying some fishy math is an obvious attempt to make the welfare problem seem even worse than it is and turn people against programs that might be more effective than critics wish to acknowledge. Whatever the case, this campaign against the welfare state relies on you failing to connect the dots, apply common sense and do the math for yourself, so you'll think the problem is far worse than it is.[3]

As for equine spouses, if you want one, just move to Massachusetts, where the law defining marriage is so vague that animals and people can intermarry—though it is still pretty hard to get on an airplane together to fly to your honeymoon. Massachusetts allows same-sex marriage, which a few politicians think is the same as bestiality. If you're going to be a nitpicker and argue about trivial details like man, horse, whatever, then you and I just disagree. You have your truth and I have mine. All truths are valid as long as you believe them hard enough.[4]

There's nothing new about frauds, deceivers and dissemblers—the original sophists were ancient Greeks, after all. What is new is the ability to spread sophistry—whether political propaganda, anti-wrinkle cream, the diet secrets of the stars, how you're getting ripped off on car insurance or three reasons to spend all your savings buying gold now!—to millions of people a day at almost no cost, with no filters, under the guise of authority. The advent of TV and the mass media in the twentieth century created a new ability to reach people everywhere, in real time. But it was expensive since you either needed to own a media outlet or pay to advertise on one. The Internet changed that, allowing virtually anybody to establish a media presence and reach others based on the mere popularity of their message, especially if they have a knack for the dark art of "going viral" and persuading thousands of others to help spread the word.

Dictators have always used propaganda to brainwash their subjects, convincing some with their hogwash while simply persuading many others to change the channel. (In North Korea—the world's

most authoritarian and broken country—the most popular TV programs aren't the official hagiographies that dominate state TV but
South Korean broadcasts watched illegally on smuggled Chinese sets
at the risk of imprisonment or death.[5]) Thanks to the miracle of the
Internet, you no longer need a propaganda ministry to brainwash the
masses; you don't even need to be a dictator. You just need to come up
with clever lies that sound true to people who want them to be true,
and circulate them via emails, blogs, Facebook posts, online town hall
meetings and other forums that make it seem like somebody knows
what they're talking about. Before the Internet, a relatively small
group of news organizations served as a filter for most information
that became public, checking that most of it was more or less true.
Now there's vastly more information available, most of it unverified.
The pathogenic propaganda infesting this information flow is a major
threat to our intellectual and economic freedom. People who believe
bogus information make bad decisions and fall behind because the
world doesn't operate the way they think it does. As their freedom de-
teriorates, they usually conclude somebody stole their freedom, while
failing to realize they forfeited it themselves. "A little learning is a
dang'rous thing," the satirical English poet Alexander Pope wrote
in the early 1700s. Nothing about the digital age has changed the
advantage the informed have over the ignorant.

There's been a terrific free-market response to the mass circula-
tion of lies. Fact-checking Web sites such as Snopes, Politifact and
others have arrived to meet the growing need to debunk. And it is
quite a contest between the liars and the debunkers, similar to the
battles between bacteria-killing cleansers and "superbugs" that evolve
to be resistant to those cleansers. At last check, Politifact gave nearly

250 public claims its lowest rating, "Pants on Fire," meaning they were total fabrications. Some of these bogus claims are anonymous chain emails or unsigned blog posts, but the majority come from the mouths of public officials or interest groups bearing some semblance of authority. Hundreds of other claims investigated by Politifact ring in as mostly false, half false or too convoluted to make sense of. Americans, meanwhile, say they have become more and more skeptical of what they read and hear. Yet lies still influence how people think and interfere with intellectual freedom, no matter how outlandish the claim. That translates into political power for the liars and a loss of political freedom for those who are duped.

Nearly 40 percent of Americans believe death panels actually exist, for instance.[6] One-fourth of American voters think Barack Obama was born outside the United States and somehow hoodwinked election boards into accepting a phony birth certificate.[7] About one-quarter of Americans don't believe the earth is warming, even though NASA has data showing that to be the case going back more than a century.[8] And—one of my favorites—nearly half of Americans think China has eclipsed the United States as a world power, even though China's GDP per capita is less than one-fifth what it is in America and China's communist government has to pump money into many major industries to keep them afloat.[9] Every one of these untruths factors in some kind of political debate. Voters who believe these lies are the ultimate losers, because they lend their support to phantom causes while sacrificing the leverage to demand policies that might genuinely make them better off.

Most people think mass misinformation is somebody else's problem. It's not. It's everybody's problem. Even careful thinkers subscribe to bogus ideas sometimes, often with ruinous results. The sham investment manager Bernard Madoff lost more than $50 billion of individuals' money not because he persuaded thousands of semi-senile grandparents to turn over their Social Security checks to him, but because at least 15 hedge funds trusted Madoff to manage money they had raised from their own wealthy clients. Hedge fund managers aren't exactly bumpkins drumming up clients at the county fair. They're among the shrewdest investors in the business, with wealthy clients who themselves tend to be adept at picking winning investments and shunning the losers. This is how dangerous the Liberty Trap can be: Even people with top education and terrific technical training are susceptible to believing what they want to believe, which in this case cost thousands of people several billion dollars' worth of financial freedom.

Many Madoff investors who lost money felt too humiliated to admit they had basically bought into a Ponzi scheme and never identified themselves publicly. But one Madoff victim who did come forward is Stephen Greenspan, a psychology professor at the University of Connecticut and an expert on dupes who wrote a book—before losing 30 percent of his retirement fund to Madoff—called *Annals of Gullibility*. That's right: an expert on gullibility turned out to be highly gullible to an epic con man. In an interview, Greenspan explained to me that gullibility comes from "trust in combination with some form of stupidity." That stupidity might be a low IQ, but it can also be present in someone with a high IQ who lacks knowledge of some specific thing (such as investing techniques) and doesn't bother to learn what he doesn't know. That makes hubris and arrogance forms of gullibility, which in turn makes a lot of successful people vulnerable to bogus information. Credit Greenspan's humility: He wrote a long article in the *Wall Street Journal* using his professional knowledge of gullibility to deconstruct his own. "In my own case," he wrote, "trust and niceness were accompanied by an occasional tendency toward risk-taking and impulsive decision-making, personality traits that can also get one in trouble."[10]

The digital revolution has made a wondrous amount of information available to anybody with an Internet connection. But it has also made it harder to figure out which information is important and which is fraudulent. The cost of having an almost limitless amount of information available is that ordinary people must bear the burden—in time, mental energy and money—of drawing meaning from it all. This is a vastly underappreciated challenge that has left millions of people wondering why an explosion of resources has left them feeling more confused and left out than ever. People are being drawn into the Liberty Trap by something that is supposed to be liberating: more information about everything going on around us.

The Internet is supposed to be a great equalizer that gives ordinary people information once held only by insiders. Everybody knows the invoice price of a new car at the dealership these days, which supposedly eliminates the information advantage the dealer used to have. Being able to compare airfares from every big carrier on a single Web site gives travelers access to privileged information only travel agents used to know. Yet the "democratization of information," as it is known, is a myth. What's really going on is more like an information arms race that ordinary people are losing. Looking stuff up on the Internet doesn't make you smarter; it just keeps you even with everybody else who can do the same thing. People who genuinely need an information advantage pay for much better data than you can get via Google and use data-mining techniques more advanced than most people employ. Serious financial traders spend gobs of money on subscription data services and superfast computers able to process information in nanoseconds and provide an infinitesimal but crucial edge over the next guy. Marketers gather every conceivable bit of data about consumers and use sophisticated software—plus actual trained data analysts—to get inside our heads in order to sell us stuff before we know we want it. Journalists like me beg and scrounge for detailed proprietary data from sources that spend a lot of money to produce it. On a personal note, I subscribe to several periodicals I trust to sort out complex matters I need to know about, and I also pay an annual fee for online access to *Encyclopaedia Britannica* so I have a reliable source of historical and biographical information for projects such as this book, my kids' homework and times when I just want to know something. Wikipedia isn't good enough.

Most people don't feel they need an information advantage because they're comfortable knowing a little. Like the comforts that lure us into the Liberty Trap and keep us there, a little bit of information is enough to help us form an opinion and persuade ourselves we know how the world works. The minimum baseline—Google—seems adequate. Google organizes all the world's information—right?—and gives us plenty of choices on any given Web search so we can find the information that best suits whatever we're looking for. And it's easy. You don't have to work very hard to do a Google search, which allows you to do to a little research on the Internet, take a nap, catch some TV and speak with familiarity about anything you might feel the need to know about.

The problem is, data warriors are armed with way more information, which is how you play a winning hand these days if you're determined to get ahead. If you believe we live in a knowledge economy in which intellectual capital is the reigning currency—and it's hard to believe otherwise—then you ought to recognize the value of investing in quality information. Francis Bacon said "knowledge is power" in the early 1600s. Knowledge has only become more powerful since then. Good information gives you an edge and helps you find opportunities not obvious to all, especially if others don't have it (and you came by that information legally); bad information leads you away from opportunity. We all have the freedom to squander the opportunity that comes from knowledge, and far too many of us exercise that freedom.

There are little lies and big lies. The little ones might seem harmless, but they breed bad habits that make us more susceptible to the big ones. We grow accustomed to getting our information from like-minded pontificators who say what we want to hear while dismissing information that makes us feel uncomfortable, even if it's true. We accept assertions that show up conveniently in our email inbox or flow out of the TV, without looking harder for less convenient information. Most of all, we expect good information to be freely available, like air, without realizing we might be absorbing noxious fumes. Like somebody who develops emphysema from breathing pollutants, we compromise intellectual health by feeding our brains toxins.

Forfeiting intellectual freedom impairs financial freedom because we make choices that set us back, mistakenly thinking they will help us get ahead. And it interferes with political freedom by making us dependent on information supplied by others to further their own interests—with little or no regard for the common good. Here are four prominent falsehoods of the digital age that contribute directly to declining living standards:

I'm worth more than that. Many of us think that whatever amount of money we earned in the best-paid year of our careers is what we deserve to make every year, and then some. The basic premise is that you only move upward in life, never sideways or downward. If somebody once paid you $100,000 per year, then you are worth at least $100,000 per year every year and you should accept nothing less. If suddenly nobody is willing to pay you $100,000 per year, then there's a problem with the system, not with you, and somebody needs to fix it.

Except nobody will fix it, because your value as a worker today isn't based on your value yesterday, no matter how much you wish it were. Economists sometimes call this the "just price" theory, which is the idea that certain things should never be priced below a certain level. The problem is, with most things, there's no agreement about what the just price ought to be, and it's usually in somebody else's interest to drive the price as low as possible. Since we live in a capitalist system, more or less, the market determines the price. Each one of us, as a worker, is nothing more than a product for sale in the marketplace for labor. It's not hard for us to understand that some consumer products lose value over time because demand for them declines, or those products simply become obsolete. The Sony Walkman (with Mega Bass!) that I thought was really cool in 1990 cost about $150, but nobody would pay a dime today for such a bulky, battery-powered contraption. Worker skills erode the same way if you never do anything to update or sharpen them. Unfortunately, this is sometimes an earth-shattering revelation to people with commonplace abilities that are plentiful in the marketplace for labor. When there's an oversupply of labor or declining demand for it, pay drops, job security disintegrates and it gets harder to find work. Liberty, not surprisingly, dissipates.

Before the digital revolution, this was less of a problem because most industries didn't change nearly as fast as they do now. People could glide along on one set of skills for a long time, which created the illusion that upward mobility was automatic. It has never been automatic, and a more turbulent economy now generates more downdrafts and crosswinds than most workers experienced a generation ago. If you know you'll be flying in rough weather, you take precautions, allowing plenty of room to recover if you suddenly lose altitude. If you expect your income throughout your career to go up and down, with occasional fallow transition periods when you need to learn something new, you'll probably live well within your means and keep some extra money set aside. Nearly two decades into the digital revolution, however, most people don't do this, instead committing themselves to homes and cars that get costlier, even as incomes stagnate.

Life was easier back then. Maybe it was, if you're one of the people who finds no use for modern marvels such as productivity apps, GPS and streaming video. But yearning for the olden days is a hallmark of people who simply find it troublesome to change.

Again, I'll use my own profession as an example. I spent the first 10 years of my career as a journalist at a weekly magazine that no longer exists. I loved it and still think of it as a wonderful experience. It became a lot less wonderful, however, as digital publishing revealed the many inefficiencies in an old print industry that hadn't changed much for nearly a century. My company began to lose money and shed staff. A polarity developed among journalists everywhere. Some complained constantly about all the changes, which they felt were ruining the news business. As the whole industry downsized, they were the ones usually shown the door. Others found it exciting because you could do all kinds of things online you couldn't do in a traditional print or broadcast setting. Nobody could control what was happening to our business, but every one of us could control our own attitude toward the changes, and either lament the transformation or do our best to understand it and look for new opportunities.

Some of the changes turned out to be good, some bad. But the most remarkable thing was the explosion in productivity for those who learned how to use the newly available tools. At the magazine, I wrote about one story a week, on average, and spent a lot of time going from place to place meeting with people and seeking story ideas, information and documentation. A decade later—after a lot of industry turmoil—I was writing six to eight stories per week, with an astounding amount of information showing up almost automatically by email every day. Likewise with writing books. Somewhere in my attic, I still have half a dozen weighty boxes filled with documentation I gathered for the first book I wrote, which came out in 2006. Now most of my book research ends up in electronic form on a computer, where it's far easier to store, track and analyze. It's no exaggeration to say my personal productivity has tripled during the last 15 years or so, allowing me to do more quality work in less time and to try new things. On the whole, new technology has enhanced, not hampered, my temporal freedom by allowing me to do more in less time.

Modern technology is a lot less appealing if it overwhelms you or makes something you're good at obsolete. But anybody who expects the economy to stand still, just for their sake, may as well ask the ocean to remain calm during a storm. There have been earlier times when the economy was, perhaps, more gentle than it is today, but there were also times when it was far more cruel. The economy itself is never a constant. What is a constant is the primacy of adaptation: Those who are good at it tend to excel in any environment. Those who are bad at it suffer.

Average is destiny. Convincing data shows that American schoolkids know less than their peers from most other advanced nations, and they're getting dumber, not smarter.[11] Median household income in the United States has been stagnant for 15 years.[12] The poverty rate in the United States is the worst of any nation in the developed world.[13] And of course the obesity rate in the United States is one of the highest in the world as well, even though we spend far more on health care per person than any other country.[14]

These are all serious problems. But no individual is ever doomed to be average, median or mediocre. We do that to ourselves—and to our kids. America's decline, if it is actually happening, as some gloomy statistics suggest, doesn't foretell any individual American's fate. Anybody looking for an excuse to explain underwhelming performance certainly has one. Many, actually: America isn't as prosperous as it once was, all the jobs have moved to China, computers have obliterated the need for humans, schools are failing their students, popular culture is a booty-filled wasteland. If you'd rather be an upper outlier, on the other hand, it's as possible as ever, and simply setting your sights on such a goal will get you halfway there. You might even discover that the competition is pretty weak—since so many people have thrown in the towel.

The anecdotal is universal. If it's been a cold winter, global warming can't possibly exist. There's an epidemic of school abductions because I heard about two just last week on CNN. Shark attacks are becoming more common. I know the president lied about the improving economy because I got turned down for a raise this year. Inflation's out of control because the price of ground beef went up. Food stamps are a scam because I saw somebody buying Twinkies with them.

We live in a world in which personal observations carry far too much importance. Sure, we should all plan our lives based on circumstances as we find them, but we would help ourselves immensely if we better understood that one or two data points don't constitute proof of anything. Instead, we assume far too frequently that local conditions are the same as national conditions, that scientific research can't be true if it contradicts what we see with our own two eyes, and that some terrible event we see on the news is bound to happen in our own backyard any day now. We are suspicious of context, subtlety and proportion as if these are the tools of charlatans. What we often fail to realize is that the flood of information that submerges every moment of consciousness these days makes random and even rare events seem commonplace. Shootings get so much saturation coverage on cable TV and online news sites that many Americans think violent crime is exploding when the opposite is true—gun crime has dropped sharply during the last 20 years.[15] Scandals involving politicians, business leaders and celebrities get saturation coverage these days, as if public depravity is something new rather than a timeless attribute linking Ben Franklin to FDR to JFK to Bill Clinton. And a phenomenon that might be called the asymmetry of bad news leads many people to react far more strongly when they hear about something going wrong—such as a crime occurring or gas prices rising—than when something goes right and it barely gets noticed.

Misinformed people have always made bad decisions because they think they know more than they do. "No one in this world . . . has ever lost money by underestimating the intelligence of the great masses of the plain people," the delightfully acerbic critic H. L. Mencken wrote in 1926.[16] In the 1950s, researchers at the University of Michigan tested how much ordinary Americans knew about basic civics and found that most didn't know what the different branches of government do, couldn't differentiate between political parties and couldn't identify their own representatives in Congress. (See, it wasn't so much better back then, after all.) Today, Edelman, the big public-relations firm, makes a distinction between the "general public" and the "informed public" when analyzing poll results and other types of research because points of view can be vastly different based on what people truly know, think they know or don't know at all. "Typical voters are well intentioned but grossly irrational about politics," scholar Jason Brennan argues in *Libertarianism*. "Voters are like quack doctors who want to cure pneumonia using leeches instead of penicillin. They are terrible at picking leaders who know more than they themselves do. Voters do not merely know nothing—they know *less* than nothing."[17]

This causes the nation a great deal of damage that is difficult to calculate because we don't know what things would be like if America were governed by enlightened leaders promoting sensible policies rather than cynical politicians exploiting widespread ignorance for the purpose of self-gain. Suffice to say, we could easily have better laws governing trade, taxation, immigration, health care and many other things if informed voters went to the trouble to learn relevant facts and held elected officials accountable to those facts. Instead, we have an industry of political and PR operatives who get paid way more than ordinary working people to craft lies, smear their opponents and persuade people to believe things that actually disserve their interests. Media outlets desperate for attention and too rushed to check their facts often abet the crime. "No lie is too extreme to be published," political scientists Thomas Mann and Norman Ornstein write in *It's Even Worse Than It Looks*. "Voters are inured to factual information."[18]

An aversion to factual information can be ruinous at a personal level, too, severely impairing financial and economic freedom.

People who believe the gloom and doom about America going down the tubes might be less inclined to fight for a better future and more acquiescent in their own kids' mediocrity. If you see technology as a threat because somebody you know got replaced by automation, then you might develop a hostile attitude that prevents you from harnessing the power of technology for your own benefit—something I've personally seen at least a dozen otherwise smart people do. Some people worsen a bout of unemployment by overestimating their value as workers and turning down jobs they feel are beneath them. And lest we think only boneheads base important decisions on bad information, consider that Apple cofounder Steve Jobs pursued alternative treatments for pancreatic cancer for nine months after doctors found a tumor in 2003. Friends and doctors pleaded with Jobs to have surgery and begin chemotherapy, but "as usual, he was good at willfully ignoring inputs that he did not want to process," biographer Walter Isaacson wrote. Those who knew Jobs called this sort of obstinacy his "reality distortion field" (which we'll probe more deeply in the next chapter). By the time Jobs finally turned back to mainstream medicine, the cancer had spread to his liver. Doctors did what they could, but four years later the cancer mutated and spread further, ultimately killing Jobs in 2011. Undergoing immediate surgery back in 2003 might have saved Jobs's life.[19]

Being better informed isn't that difficult. A simple start is to question anything that doesn't make sense. In fact, it's sometimes smart to question things that *do* make sense. Begin by challenging your own assumptions. One phenomenon that makes people gullible to bogus ideas is something psychologists call "confirmation bias," which makes us more inclined to believe information that fits our preexisting views and more likely to filter out contrary evidence.[20] That pretty much explains why conservatives believe what they hear on Fox News and liberals believe what MSNBC tells them, which can often be totally contradictory. Steve Jobs may have been committing confirmation bias when he dismissed the advice of mainstream doctors to have surgery—something he found abhorrent—and chose to believe that a vegan diet, acupuncture, hydrotherapy, cleansings and even a psychic might do the trick. It's not that difficult to defeat confirmation bias and prevent yourself from making poorly informed decisions, as long as you have the self-awareness to realize the condition is present. Smart CEOs combat their own biases by inviting dissent among the ranks and making sure they cultivate a climate in which disagreeing with the boss is a protected right. At less rarified levels, it's shrewd to invite others to challenge your beliefs and search for evidence that might prove you wrong when you're weighing an important decision and building a case for action.

In terms of politics, voters who like to think for themselves would be shrewd to renounce both the Democratic and Republican parties and register as independents. It's hard to understand why any sentient soul would ascribe to a single set of viewpoints from one political pole or the other rather than believing their own beliefs, without the need for binary categorization. The concepts of *liberal* and *conservative* have become false labels used to signify way more than the words themselves have the muscle to carry. Most people have liberal views about some things and conservative views about others, which maybe explains why independents affiliated with neither party have become the largest political block. The only reason for most people to belong to a given party these days is to enjoy the convenience of having somebody tell you what to think rather than figuring it out for yourself. In addition to empowering your own intellect, rejecting this failed, corrupting two-party arrangement might have the added benefit of compelling more states to hold open primaries in which anybody can vote for Republican or Democratic candidates to run in a general election, which in turn ought to produce better, more sensible candidates than the political extremists the current system delivers. That would be a start toward breaking down the ossified, cronyist two-party system, which, by the way, has no basis in the Constitution and may be a greater threat to American prosperity than any external danger. George Washington, in his farewell address after two terms as president, urged his compatriots to always put nation above party because political parties, he warned, could "become potent engines by which cunning, ambitious and unprincipled men will be enabled to subvert the power of the people, and to usurp for themselves the reins of government."[21]

Perhaps the most straightforward way to safeguard our intellectual freedom is to revert to an underappreciated three-word answer— I don't know—when confronted with vexing questions. "Knowing what you don't know is how you find out what the truth is," Greenspan, the gullibility expert, told me. The same gusher of information that can drown us in confusion also contains boundless nuggets of knowledge that allow us to learn almost anything, if we put them together the right way. You have to work at it sometimes—develop trusted sources of information, figure out how to detect devious lies, cross-check details and come to your own conclusions instead of adopting somebody else's. The reward, however, is remarkably powerful: You figure out who's lying to you. With that comes the freedom to truly make your own choices, know the real cost of those choices and understand the risks. Freedom comes from making your own choices. The alternative is entrapment.

TWELVE

HOW STEVE JOBS FUMBLED FREEDOM

STEVE JOBS WAS THE ARCHETYPAL AMERICAN, THE Thomas Edison of our time. He operated at the frontier of technology and expanded that frontier, creating boundless opportunities not just for himself but for thousands, perhaps millions, of others. The Jobs narrative is well known among old and young Americans alike, making the Apple cofounder an uncommon celebrity, famed for both accomplishment and failure. He took risks, became an enviable success, pushed too far, sacrificed some of his cherished freedoms, then succeeded even more. His ups and downs and his zeal for exploiting opportunity make Jobs an ideal case study for students of true liberty and the cause of financial freedom.

Jobs was a famous nonconformist who said whatever was on his mind and played by his own rules. He was the ultimate baby boomer, spending his career following his bliss and doing work he considered his life's calling. He attained fabulous wealth, flew on a private jet customized to his own specifications, drove a black Mercedes without license plates and had the ear of some of the world's most powerful people. He became a rock star of the technology world at a time when there was no such thing; he was adored by millions simply because of the gizmos he put on their desks and in their pockets. More than that, he made "a dent in the universe," as he once described his ambition, literally changing the world in a lasting and meaningful way. Historians rank Jobs not just with Edison but also with Ben Franklin and even Leonardo da Vinci. "The transformation in communications he [created gave] ordinary people the voice to topple mighty businesses and governments," a Harvard Business School professor gushed after his death in 2011.[1]

How did he do it? One inclination is to simply classify Jobs as a visionary genius, beyond normal comprehension, as if he just had magical intuition that can't be analyzed or quantified. But Jobs also had a knack for exploiting freedom where he found it and creating the conditions for freedom where it was absent. He occupied a frontier between established institutions and new digital territory, moving back and forth between two worlds like a furrier might have done bringing pelts to market in the 1700s, or an oil driller in the 1900s as he moved from business circles to wherever the oil was and back. As a digital pioneer, Jobs discovered tremendous opportunity but also took risks doing it. When Jobs failed, it was partly because he took freedom for granted. And he paid a high price for some of his freedoms, the same way ordinary mortals do—except with more flair and bombast.

Biographer Walter Isaacson describes the story of Steve Jobs as "the entrepreneurial creation myth writ large."[2] Many of us know the basic plot: Jobs was adopted by working-class parents and grew up in modest suburbs south of much pricier Palo Alto, California, the hub of Silicon Valley. Jobs started Apple Computer in his parents' garage in Los Altos in 1976, along with technology savant Steve Wozniak. Their first hit product was the Apple II, which helped Apple go public in 1980 at a valuation of $1.8 billion. The two cofounders and about 40 employees became instant millionaires.

The beloved Macintosh computer debuted in 1984 and featured several novelties, such as a mouse that still serves as basic computer technology today and relieved users of having to type commands in mystifying computerspeak. That was also the year of Apple's famous Super Bowl commercial, with the lone athlete conquering the mindless multitudes. The rebellious, anti-establishment image has stuck with Apple ever since. Yet Apple itself took on establishmentarian characteristics shortly after the arrival of the Mac, starting with a big corporate smackdown that led to Jobs getting fired by his own board of directors for irascible behavior and overall poor performance as a manager.[3] Jobs and Apple both struggled after that. Jobs started the unsuccessful computer company NeXT, which spent a decade trying to find customers for its costly machines. He had better success at Pixar, which he bought when it was a small computer graphics company, and became CEO just as *Toy Story* was about to become the studio's first big hit in 1995. Apple, meanwhile, drifted into a string of forgettable products, lost its cachet and by the mid-1990s was losing money and looking like a confused company that might not make it to the twenty-first century.

What happened next almost perfectly fits the motif of the American comeback saga. Apple brought Jobs back as an "adviser" who was soon bent on displacing the CEO and regaining control of the company he had cofounded.[4] He did exactly that, becoming iCEO (for interim) in 1997, and eventually the permanent CEO. Jobs killed extraneous products such as printers and servers, refocused the company and started turning out fetching machines like the iMac and the iBook. (The *i* was meant to emphasize seamless integration with the Internet, if you believe the crafty Jobs wasn't tweaking the narcissistic *I* society.)[5] Jobs then saw opportunities others didn't in the music, smartphone and tablet industries, which led to the iPod, the iTunes store, the iPhone and the iPad. Along the way, he also built a chain of gorgeous retail boutiques modeled on Japanese Zen gardens that helped sell even more Apple products, bucking the conventional wisdom that all retail was moving to the Web. By the time Jobs died in 2011, he had rebuilt Apple from a has-been brand into the world's most valuable technology company.

The Jobs legend—the determined visionary who bent industry after industry to his personal will—may have been enhanced by his untimely death, making him a martyr to the cause of individuality. Yet Jobs was a conflicted and in some ways tormented character—the Everyman myth writ large, if you will—whose story is more complicated than the cheery surface version the protagonist himself wanted us to believe. Genius aside, Jobs made many mistakes, blamed them on others, treated people horribly and—only grudgingly, over time— came to recognize his own flaws and limitations. Steve Jobs the legend is a terrible role model because virtually nobody possesses the unique array of talents that allowed Jobs to flourish despite boundless arrogance and excessive faith in his own abundant abilities. But there's a lot we can learn from Steve Jobs the mortal because he attained an astonishing degree of freedom, created it for others, lost it for himself and spent a decade struggling to recapture it—which he did, and then some. He entered the Liberty Trap and then blasted out of it. Three particular elements of Jobs's quest to put a dent in the universe illustrate the qualities critical to obtaining and keeping financial freedom:

1. Location, location, location.
While Jobs and Wozniak started Apple in a garage, they were hardly two solitary geeks soldering circuit boards together in isolation. They both grew up in Silicon Valley, the 40-mile strip of California that became the birthplace of the semiconductor and the world's foremost hotbed of technology. When Jobs and Wozniak were kids, the area was dominated by men who were engineers for Hewlett-Packard and Fairchild Semiconductor and the fledgling Intel, along with defense contractors such as Lockheed and Westinghouse. Wozniak's father was a rocket scientist at Lockheed. Jobs's own parents were humbler people who ended up in the valley almost by chance. Still, his father was a mechanic who loved to tinker, and his mother worked at a technology park near Stanford University, which even then attracted technical experts from all over the world. Here's how Jobs described the environment he grew up in: "Most of the dads in the neighborhood did really neat stuff, like photovoltaics and batteries and radar. I grew up in awe of that stuff and asking people about it."[6] This was not a kid who spent his time watching cartoons or dreaming of being a sports star.

A mutual friend introduced the two upstarts when Wozniak was taking time off from college to make some money and Jobs was still in high school. It was serendipity aided by the valley's awesome technical heritage. The two bonded quickly over their love of electronics (and pranks), with Jobs becoming a kind of a Tom Sawyer ringleader figure and Woz, as everybody called him, being the technical seer who could seemingly build just about anything that plugged in. Jobs went off to college in Oregon, spent some time hanging out at a nearby commune, decided to drop out of school, went to India for a while and finally came back home to a job at Atari, the video game company. By then, Wozniak was working at Hewlett-Packard, the foundational company in the valley, while building myriad gizmos in his spare time. Jobs and Woz found themselves attending meetings of something called the Homebrew Computer Club. This was an eclectic group of engineers, technologists, hippies and assorted Bay Area counterculturists interested in the emergence of the personal computer. Despite a shaggy mien, the Homebrew group, which eventually numbered more than 100, included a number of technology pioneers who would become prime movers in the rise of both Apple and the larger computing industry.

As Jobs and Woz began to assemble computers, they'd demonstrate their progress at Homebrew gatherings, where they'd get invaluable feedback and tips on where to buy cheap parts. They also benefited from contacts they made at their day jobs, and Wozniak used his Hewlett-Packard office at night to work on his freelance creations. To be sure, Jobs and Wozniak were a rare duo with remarkable capabilities between them. But when they were finally ready to market the Apple II—the machine that put Apple on the map and made them both millionaires—they also had the crucial advantage of being able to call on a network of contacts who turned out to be instrumental players in the digital revolution that was just getting started. Had Jobs and Wozniak developed the Apple II in, say, Wisconsin or Indiana—where Jobs's parents lived for a while after they were married—it's a good bet nobody today would ever have heard of either one of them.

Jobs and Wozniak hit the jackpot in what Warren Buffett calls the "ovarian lottery," the game of chance that determines where you're born and where you grow up. It's hard to imagine a better place to have come of age, professionally, than Silicon Valley in the 1970s, especially if you were intellectually curious and open to the exciting new capabilities people more knowledgeable than you were talking about. We underestimate the importance of location in the attainment of financial freedom because we buy into the idea that the whole of America is a land of opportunity. It's not anymore, and maybe it never was. But there are pockets of terrific opportunity in America. They change over time. Silicon Valley has been the world's most important technology nucleus for going on 50 years, similar to the way New York has been a trading and financial hub, Nashville a music mecca and Houston an energy dynamo.

Most people don't start out in one of the world's opportunity zones. But pioneers usually find their way there. Elon Musk, who helped start PayPal, Tesla and SpaceX and is often characterized as the next Steve Jobs, was born in South Africa but didn't stay there. He left to attend Queens University in Canada and then the University of Pennsylvania, then enrolled in a graduate program at Stanford University, which is how he arrived in Silicon Valley. (Musk left

Stanford after just a few days to start his first company.) Facebook
founder and CEO Mark Zuckerberg grew up in the New York City
suburbs, spent some time at the elite networking club known as Harvard University and then, when it was time to turn his creation into
a full-blown company, migrated to—all together now—*Silicon Valley.* (You get the point about Silicon Valley.) It's worth keeping in
mind that you can be a brilliant success even if your boots never step
anywhere near Silicon Valley. George P. Mitchell, who invented the
revolutionary drilling technique known as fracking, was a Texan who
studied petroleum engineering in his home state and bought a big
tract of land there that ended up being his laboratory for experiment-
ing with new ways to extract oil and gas from otherwise unreach-
able rock formations. It might sound obvious, but people who create
the most financial freedom for themselves—and often, for others—
are either lucky enough to start out in the right place or determined
enough to get themselves there. And they keep moving until they
figure out where they need to be. People who stay in one unfulfilling
place, by contrast, are gambling that opportunity will come to them.
Odds are, it won't.

2. The power of big institutions.

Steve Jobs was famously nonconformist, an "antimaterialistic hippie,"
as Isaacson called him. Part of the reason he became a cultural hero
(or, perhaps, antihero) was that he truly did think differently, giving
people products that made them feel good when the rest of corporate America was relentlessly focused on efficiency, uniformity and
whatever else could push costs as low as possible. Jobs felt contempt
for big companies and other institutions that squashed individuality,

an ethos evident every time somebody started a Macintosh and was greeted by its "welcome" message. No other machine did that. People embraced Jobs because he gave the finger to the establishment, which his many fans probably wanted to do but didn't dare.

The rich irony is that Jobs was a huge beneficiary of the very establishment he mocked and disdained. He flourished on the backs of large organizations such as Hewlett-Packard and the other big technology companies that formed the Silicon Valley ecosystem Jobs thrived in. Apple's creation was a team effort backed indirectly by the valley's corporate power and wealth—the same corporate infra-structure Jobs desperately sought to disrupt. Jobs may have shunned the hierarchical dictates of corporate culture, but he didn't find free-dom in being a loner or a malcontent, either. He managed to harness institutional power in ways that were far more productive than the institutions themselves were able to do, ultimately creating his own institutions—most notably, Apple Computer—that functioned the way he wanted them to. For anybody seeking the virtuous blend of intellectual freedom and financial freedom that reinforce each other, Steve Jobs illustrates how to pursue idealistic goals—dreams, if you will—through ruthlessly pragmatic means.

Perhaps the signature achievement of the original Macintosh was its graphical user interface, or GUI—the combination of a mouse, an on-screen pointer and icons you click on to accomplish tasks, which was far more intuitive than the coded language users had to type into other machines to provide instructions. The GUI was such a potent innovation that it's still the dominant way people use computers more than 30 years after Jobs introduced it—remarkable staying power at a time when technological change has never been faster. Jobs gets credit for recognizing the potential of the GUI and marketing it as part of a computer aimed at ordinary consumers—but not for inventing it. Far from it. As is well known in Apple lore, Jobs actually got the idea from Xerox and either borrowed or stole it, depending on whom you ask.

Technology mavens know the tale well, but for those who don't, the copier company Xerox, which was more influential in the 1970s than it is now, developed a famous technology lab in 1970 known as the Palo Alto Research Center, or Xerox PARC. Jobs knew through a few colleagues that there were some nifty things going on at PARC, and it also turned out that an arm of Xerox was one of the early investors in Apple, before the firm went public in 1980. Jobs used that as leverage to get an inside glimpse at some of the magic that PARC researchers had under wraps. He was astonished when he saw an early version of a GUI, an innovation that hadn't occurred to him before. "It was like a veil being lifted from my eyes," Jobs recalled. "I could see what the future of computing was destined to be."[7]

Jobs ran fast with the idea. He quickly put several Apple engineers on a project to develop a GUI and poached several of the researchers who had done work on the technology at Xerox. The first Apple machine to feature a GUI was the Lisa, which went on sale in 1983 at a hefty $9,995 and quickly flopped on account of its high price and dwindling support from within Apple itself. Apple refined the GUI further for the Mac, which was far less powerful than the Lisa but debuted at a more manageable $2,495. The Mac caught on, of course, wooing users with cutesy, intuitive features such as a virtual "desktop" on the screen that mimicked an actual desktop. Computing would never be the same.

Jobs always acknowledged that the idea for a mouse and other elements of the GUI came from Xerox, while pointing out, accurately, that Apple added numerous innovations of its own that made the technology affordable and enticing to consumers. Xerox did, in fact, try to sell a commercial computer featuring its own GUI, even bringing it to market three years before the Macintosh. But the Xerox Star, as it was known, cost nearly $17,000 and was targeted at businesses that Xerox hoped would buy several of the machines and network them together. It never caught on. Jobs was the one with the insights on how to refine the GUI and package it into a machine that consumers would embrace.

At that point in his fledgling career, Jobs would have had a hard time mustering the research and development funding it took to develop something as new as the GUI. He benefited from a paternalistic organization that had the resources to fund cutting-edge innovation he couldn't. And he saw a way to capture tremendous value from a corporate innovation that the institution itself was unable to exploit. Jobs later mocked Xerox for its clumsiness. "They were copier-heads who had no clue about what a computer could do," he said. "They just grabbed defeat from the greatest victory in the computer industry. Xerox could have owned the entire computer industry."[8] Jobs would get his comeuppance when other companies, especially Microsoft and later Google, did the same thing to Apple that Apple did to Xerox—borrow liberally from its innovations. At a testy meeting with Jobs around the time of the Mac's debut, Microsoft cofounder Bill Gates described the diffusion of the Xerox GUI technology rather cleverly: "It's like we both had this rich neighbor named Xerox and I broke into his house to steal the TV set and found out that you had already stolen it," Gates said to Jobs.[9]

Individuality, for Steve Jobs, didn't come from shunning the corporate world he found stultifying. It came from conducting sneak attacks on his enemy—often while disguised as a collaborator— to gain whatever intelligence might be helpful to him. In that way, Jobs tapped every available resource. If it might help him get ahead, he didn't discriminate between institutions he approved of and those he didn't. The lessons for ordinary people today are enormous. Jobs never apologized for advantages he gained from the many institutions around him. At the same time, he had little regard for institutional solutions to any problem; instead of waiting for those, he provided his own solutions. Whether writ large or writ small, that's what many of us need to do today: Take what we can get from institutional society, figure out the rest for ourselves and spend little effort trying to bend the steel of well-established traditions. Many of us have grown accustomed to the idea that if you care about civic, social and moral issues, you need to be either liberal or conservative, then live according to a fixed set of principles. Steve Jobs shows otherwise. He was a man of uncomfortably strong opinions who always came down in favor of ruthless pragmatism. He was a wizard at accomplishing what others couldn't, and he showed that ruthless pragmatism holds far more power than dogmatic, single-minded certainty.

3. The perils of reality distortion.

Steve Jobs had some glaring weaknesses, and the most prominent may have been his reality distortion field. We all have a reality distortion field. Many people tend to overestimate their own abilities and then fail to understand why bosses or employers don't reward them the way they feel they deserve. Academic studies show that people in positions of authority tend to overestimate their moral virtue, which helps explain why some CEOs and Wall Street barons find nothing wrong with huge paychecks for themselves that others find abhorrent.[10] There's even evidence that reality distortion can generate something called "positive illusion," which allows some people to be more optimistic about their prospects than might be the case if there were a Truth Machine telling them how they really measured up. The reason it's a positive illusion, and not a negative one, is that a measured amount of self-inflation can help some people take chances they wouldn't otherwise take and benefit from simply pushing themselves to accomplish challenging goals.[11]

If you're going to have a big reality distortion field, it's really helpful to be a GVB—genius visionary billionaire. And if you're not a GVB, then your reality distortion fields needs to be pretty small, because even GVBs can find their freedom crimped when they sidestep reality. Steve Jobs probably benefited from positive illusion, but he also suffered from negative illusion—imagining he could overcome problems that, in reality, he couldn't. If Steve Jobs forfeited freedom by fooling himself, which he did, is it possible you and I could fall into the same trap? Hmmm. Seems to bear considering.

Steve Jobs mostly compromised his intellectual and psychological freedom by overestimating his own very large abilities and, for a while, fooling himself. First, he got fired from the company he founded because he was a lousy manager who mistakenly considered himself to be impervious to authority. The Mac, introduced in 1984, was a hit, but not quite the runaway success the iPhone and other technology grand slams have been. By 1985, Mac sales had tapered off and Jobs lost the invulnerability that comes with standout performance. On top of that, Jobs had become churlish and dictatorial. He often berated those who disagreed with him, calling them "asshole" and "shit." Perhaps worse, he bathed infrequently and offended many who knew him with strong body odor. In corporate terms, Jobs lost the support of key people at Apple and the allies who usually enabled his ferocious individuality. When he finally left Apple, the company's stock price rose as investors expressed relief that infighting involving Jobs finally seemed to be over.

Twenty years later, Jobs described the experience of getting fired from Apple as "the best thing that could ever have happened to me."[12] Everybody feels that way when they get fired, right? What? Not exactly? Well, it took Jobs, like most people, a long time to find the upside in his downward momentum. And it might never have happened if not for at least one other humbling experience. When Jobs started NeXT after leaving Apple, he assumed that company would enjoy the same sort of triumphant beginning Apple did, so he spared no expense building an extravagant, glass-walled headquarters, hiring top talent and hosting fancy retreats at top resorts before the company had sold a single computer. When the company's products finally debuted, they cost $6,500 apiece, more than twice what the price should have been given the intended customers. The required software was too expensive, and it didn't do what customers needed it to do. Sales ended up at less than 10 percent of what Jobs had projected, and Jobs eventually shut down his assembly lines. In the final analysis, Jobs ended up with far too much control. "The result," Isaacson wrote, "was a series of spectacular products that were dazzling market flops." This was the comedown that forced Jobs to reevaluate his methods and made him realize his instincts weren't always right after all.

Like estranged lovers pining for a second chance, Apple and Jobs got back together after NeXT, with Jobs becoming iCEO in 1997. That turned out to be a propitious time for a computer maker desperate to figure out its next move to reconnect with a computer jock eager for a sequel. The digital revolution we readily recognize today was just getting started, and Jobs had learned enough about what doesn't work to refine his thinking, do a better job of listening to colleagues and figure out what will work in the future. NeXT had been based on the outdated premise that big, costly computers with specialized software would sell briskly to institutional clients. At NeXT, Jobs, irony of ironies, had become a dinosaur: He lost step with the pace of technology, taking years to develop elaborate machines at a time when experimental, iterative and relatively cheap computers were catching on, soon to be replaced by the next model, then the one after that.

What saved Jobs was the learned ability to recognize his mistakes, which allowed him to retool his vision and restore his own intellectual freedom. Among his many abilities, Jobs was able to reject or refine ideas he may have thought were inviolate at some point. It's something he never pointed to as a badge of honor or even as a marginal advantage. He may even have been embarrassed to admit his mistakes. Still, he made the intellectual and emotional pivot many others can't make. He acknowledged what he got wrong and changed his thinking. That can be enormously liberating. Like hockey legend Wayne Gretzky, who said, "I skate to where the puck is going to be, not where it has been," Jobs learned to focus on what was coming, not on what was already here.[13] As a result, he was able to anticipate how the iPod would be able to change the way people experienced music, the iPhone would change the way people communicated and the iPad would fill gaps left open by PCs and laptops. The ability to see just a wee bit further into the future than others is a remarkable power that for Jobs created artistic freedom, intellectual freedom and, needless to say, financial freedom. It's probably safe to say none of us is the next Steve Jobs, but all of us can learn to exploit favorable circumstances, create them when necessary and refine our mental dexterity, as Jobs did. Even a tiny dent in the universe is worth making.

THIRTEEN

FREEDOM FOUND

IN 1974, A GENETICIST NAMED MARY-CLAIRE KING BE-
gan to research the question of whether breast cancer could be hereditary. Most medical authorities at the time—nearly all of them
men—doubted it, assuming environmental toxins and other unknown
factors were the cause. For years, they rejected King's hypothesis and
mostly ignored her work. She was a woman in a male-dominated
field, chasing a pet theory.

The medical establishment perked up, however, when King
made a major breakthrough, 17 years into her research. In 1990, she
identified a genetic marker on the seventeenth chromosome that led
to the discovery of the BRCA1 gene, which in mutated form can be
inherited from a parent, which sharply raises the odds of contracting
breast, ovarian and perhaps other types of cancer. King had shown
that cancer risk can, in fact, be hereditary, a discovery that dramatically changed research into the disease and allowed preventive

screening for certain types of cancers.[1] Actress Angelina Jolie underwent a double mastectomy because screening made possible by King's research showed she carried a defective BRCA1 gene. The surgery reduced the likelihood of Jolie getting breast cancer—like her mother, who died from it at age 56—from nearly 90 percent to less than 5 percent.[2]

You might expect King to feel scornful toward colleagues who dismissed her work early in her career, or to have an I-told-you-so attitude. But instead, she's grateful for their neglect. King says being ignored for years gave her freedom she might not have otherwise had to do tedious, painstaking research. "It can be liberating to not have expectations placed on you," she says. "If you've had 17 years to develop your evidence, then you're in a much better position to defend it well." With a laugh, she recalls the famous quip from French philosopher Simone de Beauvoir: "For a woman to be taken as seriously as a man she must be three times as effective. Happily this is not difficult."[3]

King walked right past the Liberty Trap when others would have eagerly accepted the invitation to step inside. Many of us would have cursed the indignity she endured or seen only barriers where she saw opportunity. When I hear the stories of people like King, it makes me question the times I've complained bitterly about unfairness or something that didn't go my way, and I wonder if opportunity passed by, unseen, while I was too preoccupied to notice. It has probably happened, since we all lose perspective from time to time. The rewards for mindfulness aren't obvious in an instant-gratification society. Luckily for most of us, we are not confined forever to the Liberty Trap if we unwittingly step inside. We can get out and give freedom another go. It really is a great country. Still.

My study of self-reliance began with a physical test of my survival skills. It turns out my premise was wrong. Physical skills are secondary. It's our mental and psychological preparation that determines how self-reliant we are and how free we will be. If you're awake to the world as it is—and alert to changes as they happen—you'll be able to recognize vulnerabilities, threats and opportunities. That's the hard part: seeing the opportunities and seeing the traps. Mary-Claire King saw. Not everything, but enough to make her own dent in the universe. First, she saw a scientific possibility others didn't, which required training and talent but also the intellectual freedom to imagine what others couldn't. Second, she exploited freedom where she found it, when she could have chosen instead to forfeit freedom by wallowing in the unfairness of professional snubs or letting critics prove her wrong. Americans are lucky to live in a place where freedom can still be found and harnessed. But contrary to popular belief, it doesn't usually walk in your front door and say, "I'm here! Let's party!" The burden of discovery and the duty to cultivate freedom rest upon us. Even when freedom is free, its upkeep isn't.

We have remarkable opportunities to discover and cultivate freedom, even in a challenging economic environment. But we're not doing it. We spend too much time pondering what America needs to do differently at some imaginary collective level, and not enough time on what Americans—each one of us, individually, with no guidance from government or some other phantom authority—need to do differently. There is no third party or deus ex machina that will materialize like a genie and reinstate lost freedom. Only you and I can do that. Here are six ways how:

1. Build community.

Alexis de Tocqueville, the French traveler who visited the United States and wrote two famous volumes that helped form the American identity, was astonished by the communal instincts he observed in the new world. "Americans of all ages, all conditions, and all dispositions," he wrote in *Democracy in America,* "constantly form associations. They have not only commercial and manufacturing companies, in which all take part, but associations of a thousand other kinds."[4] He went on to explain that in the aristocratic societies of Europe, the actions of a few, single, powerful people (or rather, powerful men) were the usual way something got done. In the United States, it was different. No formal aristocracy ruled. There were no lords or dukes or marquises or other hereditary noblemen who set the law and enforced it. Getting something done, even something trivial, required a bunch of people to get together, hash it out and come to an agreement. "All the citizens are independent and feeble," Tocqueville wrote. "They all, therefore, fall into a state of incapacity, if they do not learn voluntarily to help each other."[5]

Does this sound like America today? Humble people voluntarily helping each other for the common good? Umm . . . well, certainly not in Washington, not on Wall Street, not in boardrooms and not even in universities. America has developed a quasi aristocracy of its very own, which doesn't come with titles, exactly, but does come with extreme privilege, tons of inherited wealth and protective walls that are growing higher and thicker. Not so long ago, if you went to a ball game, blue-collar and white-collar fans would sit in seats right next to each other, ordering the same hot dogs and beer from the strolling vendor. Today, the wealthy sit in pricey box seats or luxury enclaves and enjoy delicacies from waiters, while everybody else occupies the bleachers. Exclusivity is the rule, class integration the exception.

We're lonelier than we used to be, too. In 2000, Harvard political scientist Robert D. Putnam published *Bowling Alone,* the now-famous book that documented various ways civic involvement had declined since the 1950s, as Americans became more apt to keep to themselves and less likely to join the sorts of voluntary associations Tocqueville marveled at. The thesis fits with economic trends. Bigger, more lavish houses give you more of an incentive to stay in and enjoy your home theater system instead of hanging out at the VFW Hall or the Elks Lodge. When rising incomes allow you to buy more stuff, you spend more time with your gizmos and less time with people. In my own life, the loner impulse might be better described as basketballing alone than as bowling alone. My teenage son has begged me to install a basketball hoop in the driveway so we can shoot hoops at home—like every other normal family, in his suburban universe—instead of rubbing elbows with the myriad sorts down at the community courts. So far I've resisted, because the comforting confines of home can trick you into losing the instinct for civic involvement. Meanwhile, I make sure my son's bike is always tuned up so he can scoot down to the park and play with the locals.

Social media and the many alleyways of the Internet have obviously changed the social equation Putnam wrote about in *Bowling Alone,* allowing us to commune online with people whose interests we share. There's nothing wrong with that, although Putnam has since pointed out that many groups that people belong to today aren't civic groups where people gather to play cards, discuss books or solve town problems, but national activist groups such as the Sierra Club, the National Rifle Association or AARP, which exist mainly to raise money and lobby for particular causes. It's less about working together on some issue that affects your life directly and more about positions you take on broader matters that form your public, but not private, identity.

I've gotten in the habit of applying a "lights out" test toward the people, things and influences in my life: What would happen if the power went out? Would that person or thing still be there in equal measure? Or would it be rendered useless? One of the most important things I learned while spending time with the preppers was the value of the community itself: people to learn from, laugh with and rely on for help when needed. A pretty basic concept, which Americans probably took for granted around the time Tocqueville came to visit. But better mobility and easier living allow us to drift away from the things that provide us genuine freedom. I guess I had lost sight of those simple virtues as I focused on raising kids, became professionally ambitious, moved around for my job and for personal reasons, and always seemed to find some project to fill up my spare time. Now, when I consider the community I inhabit and ask what would happen if the power went out, I'm not sure it's robust enough. I have terrific family and many friends, but they are spread out along the East Coast and not so nearby. If the power went out, there's little or nothing we'd be able to do for each other.

Community provides freedom because you don't have to do everything yourself. Mutual assistance plugs gaps, creates resilience and reduces single-point-of-failure problems, as an engineer might say. In this way, the phrase *self-reliance* is a bit misleading because you can end up isolated and endangered if you truly concentrate on self alone. Many selves are better. Community also provides shared resources when there's not an emergency, of course: through all kinds of support groups, online forums and, sure, social media. As a freedom-building exercise, broadening your community doesn't require radical change. All you have to do is get to know more of your neighbors, pursue an interest deeply enough to seek out others who share it, or say yes when somebody asks you to join the PTA instead of making excuses about how busy you are. Tocqueville would be pleased.

One final point about forming strong communities: It can also be a good way to improve your career prospects and therefore boost your living standards. The entire digital revolution to date hasn't changed the fact that the old tradition of networking is still the best way to develop professional contacts, stay in the loop on important professional events and learn first about opportunities that might suit you. In fact, the more mobile you are, the more important this old-fashioned type of community becomes.

2. Live in a smaller world.

A few years ago I worked with some of my neighbors to get two new stop signs installed on our street. It wasn't easy. We lived on a residential street that was bearing a lot of pass-through traffic, even though the speed limit was 25 miles per hour and there was a sign saying *No Trucks*. Vehicles sometimes sped by at twice the speed limit, and some trucks must have been going too fast for the driver to read the sign, because the trucks came as if there were no sign there at all. We had to pester city officials for about two years before they finally addressed the problem. It was clear there was a huge backlog of projects and they hoped we would just lose interest and go away. But persistence and a unified front paid off. Two stop signs eventually went up, and while they didn't keep every single truck away, traffic thinned out and slowed considerably. At our insistence, government accomplished something. It was a fulfilling moment of political freedom.

Does any ordinary citizen ever feel a sense of accomplishment when urging the federal government to do something? Professional lobbyists and interest groups certainly do, but the rest of us mostly just fulminate over events in Washington, or tune them out altogether. So why do so many people form their identities these days based on intangible matters relating to Washington politics? Why do people buy into the bogus labels and categorizations created by the political-media establishment? Why do people characterize themselves—and others—as liberal or conservative? If you're so interested in politics, why not exercise your political freedom in a real community where your feet are planted and you might be able to have an actual impact on decisions that make people's lives better?

Try to think of the issues that get most of the attention on the news, then consider the things that actually affect you in some tangible way where you live. You might feel strongly about abortion, but is it something you have to deal with every day when you drive your kids to school or head to work? Is there an illegal immigrant waiting outside your door every morning, threatening your livelihood? Does some foreign policy controversy affect your performance at work or your kids' grades? And if you really can't stand the president, does it ruin your family vacations or fishing trips or evenings out or whatever you do to unwind?

Obviously some people are, in fact, directly affected by the things that cause foaming at the mouth on cable news. But for most of us, local issues like safety and crime, cost of living, traffic, the quality of our kids' schools and the character of our neighborhoods affect us a lot more. Taxes are one big political issue that affects nearly everybody, but federal tax rates don't change much, for all the rabid jawboning they produce. State and local taxes—and especially property taxes, which affect renters, too—are more likely to change in many places. So you'd think people who are passionate about political freedom would invest most of their efforts locally, where the stakes are highest and the payoff is direct. But that's not what happens. We've become a blue-red nation riven by sharply differing viewpoints on faraway issues that will affect most people only in a diluted way, while we tend to overlook issues closer to home we might actually be able to do something about. Fussing over national politics mostly produces frustration and disenchantment, no matter which side you're on, because our national politics have become a war of attrition that benefits only the war profiteers. Anybody who has ever gotten involved in a local matter and helped determine the outcome knows that is vastly more liberating.

3. Underconsume and overproduce.

There's a saying in business: underpromise and overdeliver, a strategy designed to build a reputation as somebody who exceeds expectations. We should do the same in our lives as consumers by underconsuming and overproducing. America does the opposite, in aggregate, which is why we are indebted as a nation, at both the household and government level. You are literally indentured when you carry debt—your creditors' legal right to get paid back super-sedes your own rights and freedoms. There are legitimate reasons to take the risk debt entails. You might earn more by deploying bor-rowed money than you have to pay back in principal and interest, which is the definition of a good investment. That can obviously enhance your freedom. Sometimes emergencies leave us little choice but to take on debt to dig ourselves out of a hole. But borrowing to finance stuff we don't need or things that won't improve our lives in the long run is a one-way trip into the Liberty Trap. You may as well go to the nearest police station and turn yourself in for violat-ing the law of common sense.

Modern innovations have offered some fresh ways to live on less without compromising your living standards by much, if at all. Rent-ing a home rather than owning one carries no stigma these days, and might just indicate you're the shrewdest person in the neighborhood, able to relocate quickly if an opportunity arises or circumstances re-quire. In fact, a whole rental economy (often dubbed the "sharing economy," which is misleading since nobody's sharing for free) has sprung up to provide smart consumers the privileges usually associ-ated with owning, minus the excessive cost and hassle factor. Zipcar and other such companies rent upscale vehicles—not at the airport, where nobody lives, but in many population centers—for people who want to get away for the weekend or just need to run errands. A Web site called Rent the Runway rents designer dresses and accessories for a single occasion for about one-tenth the cost of buying. Airbnb lets you rent other people's homes for an out-of-town trip or a nearby extended stay. Other businesses rent everything from musical in-struments (for the one year your kid is required to take lessons in school) to lawn equipment. And you could probably arrange many other rental deals on your own. The risk, of course, is that instead of becoming addicted to shopping, you become addicted to renting. It's not hard to imagine a supersampler psychosis in which people go broke because they can't stop taking designer rentals for a spin. Let's hope we can count on the drug companies to develop medication for that syndrome once it develops.

That's consumption. Most of us also need to produce something to finance what we consume, and the simple—in fact, obvious—way to balance the two is to consume only what your production pays for, or less. If you want or need more, earn more first. In fact, always earn more, and save what you don't spend. If you can't earn more, figure out what you might be able to change so you can. Or survive on less. We've overcomplicated this basic equation by placing a social safety net beneath it, which has corrupted the simple idea that you should only consume in proportion to what you produce. You can live your whole life in America consuming more than you earn. People who spend their lives receiving public assistance obviously fit the profile, but you can be a lifelong overconsumer by borrowing, too, even if you never get a dime in public subsidies. Wherever the funny money comes from, the fact that consumption and production don't have to be balanced has created deep distortions in the way we finance our lives. I'm not a heartless, laissez-faire capitalist who thinks we should abolish the safety net and force everybody to fend for themselves. It's good the net is there. Some people inevitably will fall into it, and we ought to catch them. But don't be one of the people who falls into the net! Do the simple math and produce more than you consume. Freedom this way lies.

4. Know your vulnerabilities.

It doesn't take a superstorm or a terrorist event to mess up your life. All kinds of things can happen that might throw you off stride. Your employer might downsize, move or shut down. You could get sick or hurt unexpectedly. A tree could crash through your roof. Divorces happen. Under the wrong circumstances, a small setback becomes a bigger one. When two things or more go wrong at once, it can snowball into a disaster. There are more than one million personal bankruptcies per year to prove it.

Well-run companies such as Google, Netflix, Starbucks and Coca-Cola have institutionalized the practice of asking what might go wrong. Good CEOs worry all the time about market risk, headline risk, tail risk and many other types of risk, most of them unpredictable. They're not doomsayers. They're cautious. Larry Page, CEO of Google, says, "The main thing that has caused companies to fail is that they missed the future."[6] They didn't see what was coming and got sideswiped when it arrived. Nobody can predict every possible eventuality, but some aren't that hard to predict or prepare for.

If you've ever been through a major setback, you probably developed a kind of reflex instinct that left you looking in the rearview mirror more often, checking your tail. After a divorce I didn't see coming, I found myself thinking constantly about what else might go wrong. Sometimes, it did. I don't think I've become downcast or paralyzed by fear, but I go out of my way to analyze every conceivable worst-case scenario when I have a decision to make. When I bought a house recently, I ran spreadsheets estimating what would happen if the uncontrollable costs such as utilities or maintenance ended up considerably higher than I anticipated, or my income ended up considerably lower. Satisfied with what I saw, I bought the house. I've turned down some jobs because the risk of something going wrong seemed too high, and accepted others because my calculations showed there was enough wiggle room to accept the risks.

Worriers get a bad rap. We are not negativists or Debbie Downers. In fact, we are freedom-loving people who feel a lot more comfortable taking risks and doing other things that create opportunity once we have asked and answered all the unpleasant questions. Anybody who craves financial freedom and wants to get ahead should assess all the things that might interfere with reaching important goals. If you've got a health issue, are you insured or otherwise prepared for what might happen? Do you have backup plans in case you lose your job? Are you maxed out on monthly bills, with no wiggle room, or can you run up credit for a while in an emergency? Perhaps most of all, who else can you depend on if you really need to? If you can answer those questions comfortably, you will have a surprising amount of freedom and you might even stop worrying for a while. (Just don't stop worrying for too long.)

5. Just say "I don't know."

This is a personal plea. Almost none of us is as smart as we think we are. Not even the smartest among us. There's a saying among some technologists: "Always certain, never right." That's how they describe people who mistakenly think they know everything necessary to know, and will never come by any new information that's relevant—as if there's some point in time at which discoveries will stop happening and our state of knowledge will be perfect. Yet there's far too much certainty in the world. People are way too sure they know things that are hard to know, and way too sure other people don't.

The geyser of information supplied by Google and its ilk has created a false sense of knowledge that can afflict just about anybody. Worse, the partisan orthodoxies that some people subscribe to have almost become like religious cults that teach a certain dogma as the one and only truth; any other idea, therefore, can only be a lie. Truth! We mock the very concept with our certainty. As a journalist who covers controversial topics from time to time, I have been commented upon by thousands of readers who insist I'm wrong and they're right; I'm misinformed and they're better informed; I'm a liar and they know the truth. And apparently I'm a shameless propagandist for both liberal and conservative causes, since the criticism comes with equal intensity from both sides. What is missing in these comments and in much of our public discourse is the simple acceptance that maybe both sides can be "right" to some extent, and there's value in the middle. Meanwhile, the smartest people of all are those who realize that actual truth is extraordinarily difficult for mere mortals to ascertain. "We absolutely must leave room for doubt or there is no progress and there is no learning," the great physicist Richard Feynman said. "People search for certainty. But there *is* no certainty."[7]

It is refreshing and liberating, on the other hand, to say "I don't know." Maybe it's a complex national issue such as tax and spending reform you don't know enough about to form an insightful opinion. Or maybe it's a vote on whether the unionized garbage collectors in your town should get a raise and a new contract. If you say "I don't know," you create no burden to prove you know what you're talking about. And you don't back yourself into a corner by having to adopt somebody else's opinion since you don't know enough to justify your own. What you do by saying "I don't know" is establish credibility for intellectual honesty (which instantly catapults you into an exalted sphere of existence) while opening the door to actually learning something. You are free when you admit what you don't know because then you can learn with nothing to prove and no agenda to fulfill. Certainty, by contrast, is a prison that can force you to bend logic itself in order to justify intellectual commitments you never should have made. Nobody should make up your mind but you, and there is no statute of limitations dictating a deadline.

6. Hug a prepper.

Before I bugged out with the preppers, I had already developed that reflex instinct compelling me to ask what could go wrong whenever I did something that involved taking a risk, or even when I was just sitting in neutral, idling. The preppers pushed me one step further. Once you identify what could go wrong, what are you going to do about it? And what are you going to do about things that might go wrong that you've never even considered?

Proportion matters here, because when it comes to prepping, there's a point of optimal return and then there are many points of diminishing return. You can easily go overboard prepping, just as a hypochondriac puts so much effort into worrying about illness that he can't enjoy being healthy. But it's well worth worrying a little. Do that, and there's no need to worry more.

These six basic guidelines, in fact, may be all the prepping most people need to achieve and sustain financial and political freedom. If you know your vulnerabilities, you're already ahead of most people and aware of the leaks that may need to be plugged if the rain comes. If you just say "I don't know," you're building the mental suppleness to adapt if something surprising happens. Underconsuming and overproducing will help you set aside resources for the day you might need them. Living in a smaller world will allow you to prioritize the things that matter most in your life and might need vital attention at some point. And building community helps you prepare for the things you can't predict because people share resources when they pull together in common cause. What you don't have your neighbor will, and vice versa.

A few months after my bug-out weekend with the preppers, I ran into Omar, who had saved or at least smothered my gloves when they caught fire in the woods, at a deli on 42nd Street in midtown Manhattan, where we were both getting a breakfast sandwich one morning. It may have taken him a moment to recognize me, but not the other way around; I could have spotted Omar's scruffy amplitude in a crowd of thousands. We bantered a bit, then he told me he had purchased a small plot of land in northern New England, far away from the types of crowds that were streaming past us just outside the deli door. He didn't yet have the money to build a house on the land, but that would come, in time.

As we walked out of the deli, he turned right and I turned left, two people plunging into the metropolis to take what we could from it and, with luck, make our lives better, bit by bit. His way of doing it wasn't mine, and mine wasn't his. But Omar's little plot of land sounded like a pretty good place to me, procured with forethought to serve a modest and pragmatic purpose—fulfilling and sustaining one man's idea of liberty, earned, not granted, through persistent dedication to the cause. It wasn't out of the question we might become neighbors someday.

ACKNOWLEDGMENTS

WRITERS ARE MOST VERBOSE WHEN THANKING PEO-
ple. I will attempt to improve upon the precedent.

I am grateful to Jess, Jeanine, Thomas and Robert, who give
my life meaning and purpose and also keep me grounded and, occasionally, humble. My impromptu lectures to all of you have often
been warm-ups for various rants later put to journalistic use. Thanks
for your tolerance when you've offered it and your hints when I've
overfulminated.

My agent, Lisa Gallagher, is a terrific business partner. Thanks
for sticking with me, Lisa.

At Palgrave, Karen Wolny took a chance on this project and gave
it the kind of care and attention you'd expect from the author himself. Karen, you made this book way better, which makes me feel
lucky as a writer. Alan Bradshaw scrutinized the manuscript with
a jewel-cutter's eye for precision and suggested dozens of improvements that make me seem smarter than I am. Bill Warhop may have
the highest batting average of any copy editor I've ever worked with,
since I agreed with about 99.4 percent of the changes and suggestions
he made. Others on the Palgrave team, including Laura Apperson,

Lauren LoPinto, Lauren Janiec, and Christine Catarino, are top-shelf pros who are great at many things I am not, which allowed me to just write. This impressive team helped turn a raw collection of ideas into a finished product better than I could have hoped for.

At Yahoo Finance, Aaron Task and Rebecca Stropoli helped me find time to work on this book when it seemed there was no time. That was tremendously helpful. The other Yahoo Finance journalists I work with daily are remarkably productive pros who push me to raise my game by their mere example. Thanks, guys.

Jason Charles was far more open and accommodating than he needed to be.

I owe large debts of gratitude to Sarah and Keifer, Lisa and Mike, Gayle and Ted, Julie and Rick, Diane and Ted, Debbie Stier and Kelly Leonard. They have backed and supported me in innumerable ways.

My Mom, Grandma Cook, is in a category of her own. Mom, you are the best grandma my two kids could have and a pretty good Mom, too. Even now.

Bob Newman, you set high standards I strive to meet decades later. You made your own dent in the universe.

Finally: I draw motivation and inspiration from many people who are probably unaware of the impressions they leave on me. I strive for mindfulness, for the grace to acknowledge people's contributions to my life in real time, but sometimes the dividend materializes well after the gift has been delivered. For all who have shaped, guided or blessed me in ways that haven't dawned on me yet, I pledge my future appreciation.

NOTES

Chapter 1

1. Carmen DeNavas-Walt, Bernadette D. Proctor, and Jessica C. Smith, "Income, Poverty, and Health Insurance Coverage in the United States: 2012," US Census Bureau, US Department of Commerce, September 2013, 33, table A-1, http://www.census.gov/prod/2013pubs/p60-245.pdf. The best hard evidence of declining living standards may be median household income, adjusted for inflation, which peaked in 1999. Income fell for several years after that and still hasn't regained the 1999 peak, which means the typical household simply has less money to spend.

Chapter 2

1. World Bank, "GDP Per Capita (Current US$)," World Bank, 2009–2013, accessed November 3, 2014, http://data.worldbank.org/indicator/NY.GDP.PCAP.CD.

2. Gordon Green and John Coder, "Household Income Trends," Sentier Research, ongoing monthly series, published privately and provided to the author.

3. Paul Wiseman, "Top 1 Percent in U.S. Took Biggest Share Since 1928," Associated Press, September 10, 2013, http://finance.yahoo.com/news/top-1-percent-us-took-174338641.html.

4. "Table 8.2—Outlays by Budget Enforcement Act: 1962–2019" and "Table 8.4—Outlays by Budget Enforcement Act Category as percentage of GDP: 1962–2019," Historical Tables, Office of Management and Budget, accessed November 3, 2014, http://www.whitehouse.gov/omb/budget/Historicals. I converted the dollar figures to current-day values using the Bureau of Labor Statistics inflation calculator at http://www.bls.gov/data/inflation_calculator.htm.

5. Kyle Pomerleau, "Summary of Latest Federal Income Tax Data," Tax Foundation, December 18, 2013, http://taxfoundation.org/article/summary-latest

-federal-income-tax-data. Approximately 137 million Americans filed a tax return in 2011, the last year for which data were available.

6. "Table 7.1—Federal Debt at the End of Year: 1940–2019," Historical Tables, Office of Management and Budget, accessed August 18, 2014, http://www.whitehouse.gov/omb/budget/Historicals.

7. Louis Jacobson, "Medicare and Social Security: What You Paid Compared with What You Get," Politifact, February 1, 2013, http://www.politifact.com/truth-o-meter/article/2013/feb/01/medicare-and-social-security-what-you-paid-what-yo/.

8. "Health Insurance Coverage of the Total Population," Kaiser Family Foundation, accessed July 23, 2014, http://kff.org/other/state-indicator/total-population/.

9. "Frequently Asked Questions About 401(k) Accounts," Investment Company Institute, accessed August 7, 2014, http://www.ici.org/policy/retirement/plan/401k/faqs_401k.

10. There's a lot of research on the deterioration of the US middle class during the last 15 years and the apparent decline of Western affluence. A few of my favorites: *The Great Stagnation* and *Average Is Over* by Tyler Cowen, *Coming Apart* by Charles Murray and *When the Money Runs Out* by Stephen D. King. You don't have to be a grim declinist or subscribe to apocalyptic theories to believe that subtle changes over time have had a pernicious effect on Western living standards.

11. "Labor Force Statistics including the National Unemployment Rate," Bureau of Labor Statistics, US Department of Labor, http://data.bls.gov/pdq/querytool.jsp?survey=ln. This is an online worksheet on which you must choose "civilian labor force participation rate" in Box 7 to retrieve the relevant data. Calculating the change in the number of Americans who might be working today requires population data from "Historical Data: 2000s," US Census Bureau, http://www.census.gov/popest/data/historical/2000s/index.html. The estimated US population for 2015 is 321 million, according to "2012 National Population Projections: Summary Tables," US Census Bureau, http://www.census.gov/population/projections/data/national/2012/summarytables.html. Labor force data are for Americans aged 16 and older. All data accessed August 18, 2014.

12. Justin McCarthy, "In U.S., 65% Dissatisfied with How Gov't System Works," Gallup, January 22, 2014, http://www.gallup.com/poll/166985/dissatisfied-gov-system-works.aspx.

13. "As Sequester Deadline Looms, Little Support for Cutting Most Programs," Pew Research Center for the People and the Press, February 22, 2013, http://www.people-press.org/2013/02/22/as-sequester-deadline-looms-little-support-for-cutting-most-programs/1/.

2. "Bills, Resolutions," Library of Congress, http://thomas.loc.gov/home/bills
_res.html. I arrived at this tally by using the search tool and searching for
the terms *liberty* and *freedom* in the name or summary (but not the full text)
of legislation introduced in the 113th Congress, as of December 31, 2013.

3. Light Bulb Freedom of Choice Act, H.R. 849, 112th Congress (2011),
https://www.govtrack.us/congress/bills/112/hr849.

4. "History of Vaccine Safety," Centers for Disease Control, accessed March
16, 2014, http://www.cdc.gov/vaccinesafety/vaccine_monitoring/history
.html.

5. Nina Shapiro, "With Fewer Vaccinations, Is Your Child's School Safe?,"
Los Angeles Times, August 10, 2013, http://www.latimes.com/news/opinion
/opinionla/la-oe-shapiro-schools-and-vaccination-rates-20130811,0,37
43127.story#ixzz2lLD1W1Sh. Contrary to what you might expect, the
"anti-vax" movement seems to be just as prominent among the wealthy as
among the poor.

6. "77% of Americans Feel Firearm Rights Should Come with Some Re-
strictions; 14% Favor No Limitations," Harris, April 1, 2014, http://www
.harrisinteractive.com/NewsRoom/HarrisPolls/tabid/447/mid/1508
/articleId/1405/ctl/ReadCustom%20Default/Default.aspx; "Guns," Gallup,
October 3–6, 2013, http://www.gallup.com/poll/1645/guns.aspx. Americans are split on whether laws regulating the purchase and use of firearms
ought to be strengthened. Support for tougher gun laws typically goes up
following news of mass shootings, then declines. But on the basic question
of whether Americans should have the right to own guns, a majority consistently says yes, as these and other polls show.

7. Rick Newman, "When Americans Took Pride in Paying Taxes," *U.S. News
& World Report,* November 28, 2012, http://www.usnews.com/news/blogs
/rick-newman/2012/11/28/when-americans-took-pride-in-paying-taxes.

8. Dan Amira, "Senator Lindsey Graham Says Avoiding Taxes Like
Mitt Romney Is 'Really American,'" *New York,* July 11, 2012, http://ny
mag.com/daily/intelligencer/2012/07/lindsey-graham-taxes-romney
.html.

9. Eduardo Porter, "America's Aversion to Taxes," *New York Times,* August 14,
2012, http://www.nytimes.com/2012/08/15/business/economy/slipping-be
hind-because-of-an-aversion-to-taxes.html?_r=1. This includes state and local levies as well as federal taxes.

10. "US Business Cycle Expansions and Contractions," National Bureau of Economic Research, accessed June 4, 2014, http://www.nber.org/cycles.html.
Since World War II, there's been an economic downturn every six years or so,
lasting 11 months on average. In the half century before the Federal Reserve
came into existence, there was a downturn every four years with an average

duration of 23 months. The 1800s were an exciting time for America, but
tend to forget how frequent and devastating recessions and depressions we

11. I am hardly exaggerating in terms of the evils Obamacare critics have claim
will result from the law. For a list of such claims, page through some of
public statements on health care deemed "false" at fact-checking site Pol
fact: http://www.politifact.com/subjects/health-care/.

12. "Public Approval of Health Care Law," Real Clear Politics, accessed Ju
8, 2014, http://www.realclearpolitics.com/epolls/other/obama_and_de
crats_health_care_plan-1130.html. This is an aggregation of several po
asking people whether they favor or oppose the health care law.

13. Jeffrey M. Jones, "One in Four U.S. Uninsured Plan to Remain That W
Gallup, December 3, 2013, http://www.gallup.com/poll/166115/one-fe
-uninsured-plan-remain.aspx.

14. Jason Brennan, *Libertarianism: What Everyone Needs to Know* (New Yo
Oxford University Press, 2012), Kindle edition, Chapter 1, Question 12.

15. "Confidence in Institutions," Gallup, accessed August 22, 2014, http
www.gallup.com/poll/1597/confidence-institutions.aspx#3.

16. Ron Fournier and Sophie Quinton, "In Nothing We Trust," *National Journ
April 19, 2012, http://www.nationaljournal.com/features/restoration-ca
/in-nothing-we-trust-20120419.

17. Carmen DeNavas-Walt, Bernadette D. Proctor, and Jessica C. Smith, Ta
A-1, "Income, Poverty, and Health Insurance Coverage in the United Stat
2012," US Census Bureau, US Department of Commerce, September 20
33, http://www.census.gov/prod/2013pubs/p60-245.pdf.

18. Pew Research Center's Journalism Project Staff, "The New Washingt
Press Corps," Pew Research Journalism Project, July 16, 2009, http://ww
.journalism.org/2009/07/16/new-washington-press-corps/.

19. "State and County QuickFacts," US Census Bureau, accessed March 7, 20
http://quickfacts.census.gov/qfd/states/11000.html; "GDP by Metro Are
Bureau of Economic Analysis, US Department of Commerce, access
March 7, 2014, http://www.bea.gov/newsreleases/regional/gdp_metro/g
_metro_newsrelease.htm.

20. Thomas E. Mann and Norman J. Ornstein, *It's Even Worse Than It Loo
(New York: Basic Books, 2012), 36.

21. Ibid., 33.

22. "Party Affiliation," Gallup, accessed April 24, 2014, http://www.gall
.com/poll/15370/party-affiliation.aspx.

23. Mann and Ornstein, *It's Even Worse Than It Looks,* 103.

24. I'm borrowing some of these ideas on political versus personal identity fro
New York Times columnist David Brooks, in particular this column: Dav
Brooks, "The Stem and the Flower," *New York Times,* December 2, 201

/pageviewer-idx?cc=ecco;c=ecco;idno=004839390.0001.002;node=004839 390.0001.002%3A141.1;seq=430;page=root;view=text.

16. Lindsey Sharpe, "Americans' Life Ratings Improve in November," Gallup, December 9, 2013, http://www.gallup.com/poll/166166/americans-life-rat ings-improve-november.aspx.

17. Schmidtz and Brennan, *Brief History of Liberty*, 224.

18. "Freedom in the 50 States," Mercatus Center at George Mason University, accessed April 14, 2014, http://freedominthe50states.org/.

19. "Crime in the United States, 1993–2012," Uniform Crime Reports, Federal Bureau of Investigation, accessed September 9, 2014, http://www.fbi .gov/about-us/cjis/ucr/crime-in-the-u.s/2012/crime-in-the-u.s.-2012/tables /1tabledatadecoverviewpdf/table_1_crime_in_the_united_states_by_vol ume_and_rate_per_100000_inhabitants_1993-2012.xls. In 1993, the nationwide violent crime rate was 747 crimes per 100,000 people. In 2012, it was 387.

20. Jeffrey M. Jones, "Same-Sex Marriage Support Solidifies Above 50% in U.S.," Gallup, May 13, 2013, http://www.gallup.com/poll/162398/sex-mar riage-support-solidifies-above.aspx.

21. Stephen D. King, "When Wealth Disappears," *New York Times*, October 6, 2013, http://www.nytimes.com/2013/10/07/opinion/when-wealth-disappe ars.html?pagewanted=1&_r=0.

22. "Thomas Piketty's 'Capital,' Summarised in Four Paragraphs," *Economist*, May 4, 2014, http://www.economist.com/blogs/economist-explains/2014/05/ec onomist-explains; Thomas Piketty, *Capital in the Twenty-First Century*, trans. Arthur Goldhammer (Cambridge, MA: Harvard University Press, 2014).

23. Brennan, *Libertarianism*, Chapter 6, Question 68.

24. Martin Gilens and Benjamin I. Page, "Testing Theories of American Politics: Elites, Interest Groups, and Average Citizens," *Perspectives on Politics*, September 2014, http://bit.ly/1nUgJnD.

Chapter 6

1. "Wash. State Man Lost in Woods Gets Blessing in Disguise from Ordeal," *ABC News*, December 17, 2013, http://gma.yahoo.com/blogs/abc-blogs /wash-state-man-lost-woods-gets-blessing-disguise-115019536—abc-news -topstories.html.

2. Ron Chernow, *Washington: A Life* (New York: Penguin Press, 2010), 31–35.

3. Ibid., 328–30, 372–73.

4. Jeffrey Toobin, "Our Broken Constitution," *New Yorker*, December 9, 2013, 64–73, http://www.newyorker.com/magazine/2013/12/09/our-broken-cons titution.

5. "Respectfully Quoted," Bartelby.com, accessed September 9, 2014, http:// www.bartleby.com/73/1593.html.

6. Sarah Green, "10 Extraordinary People and Their Lessons for Success," *Harvard Business Review*, HBR Blog Network, December 30, 2013, http://blogs.hbr.org/2013/12/10-extraordinary-people-and-their-lessons-for-success/.

7. Toobin, "Our Broken Constitution," 64.

8. Philip Rucker and David A. Fahrenthold, "After Wrangling, Constitution Is Read on House Floor, Minus Passages on Slavery," *Washington Post*, January 7, 2011, http://www.washingtonpost.com/wp-dyn/content/article/2011/01/06/AR2011010602807.html.

9. Toobin, "Our Broken Constitution," 64.

10. Henry Clay, "In defence of the American system, against the British colonial system," 1832, OpenLibrary.org, https://archive.org/stream/cihm_44022#page/n39/mode/2up. The reference to "self-made men" is on the page labeled 20.

11. Benjamin Franklin, *Poor Richard's Almanack* (New York: Skyhorse Publishing, 2007), Kindle edition, 28.

12. Robert N. Bellah, "Individualism and Commitment in American Life," Santa Barbara Lecture Series, University of California, February 20, 1986, http://www.robertbellah.com/lectures_4.htm.

13. Alexis de Tocqueville, *Democracy in America*, vol. 2, trans. Henry Reeve, Kindle public domain edition, Chapter X, final paragraph.

14. Ibid., Chapter II, first paragraph.

15. Ibid., Chapter II, final paragraph.

16. Ibid., Appendix Z.

17. Ralph Waldo Emerson, "Self-Reliance," Emersoncentral.com, 1841, http://www.emersoncentral.com/selfreliance.htm.

18. Frederick Douglass, "Self-Made Men," Frederick Douglass Heritage, 1871, http://www.frederick-douglass-heritage.org/self-made-men/.

19. Bellah, "Individualism and Commitment in American Life."

20. Kenneth J. Winkle, "Abraham Lincoln: Self-Made Man," *Journal of the Abraham Lincoln Association* (Summer 2000): 1-16, http://hdl.handle.net/2027/spo.2629860.0021.203.

21. Frederick Jackson Turner, "The Significance of the Frontier in American History," *Proceedings of the State Historical Society of Wisconsin*, December 14, 1893, http://xroads.virginia.edu/~HYPER/TURNER/. This essay was later included in the book *The Frontier in American History*, published by Henry Holt in 1920. Turner earned a posthumous Pulitzer Prize for his work as a historian in 1933.

22. Joseph McLaughlin, "Real Men Don't Each Quiche, or Do They?," Fordham University news release, March 2011, http://www.fordham.edu/campus_resources/enewsroom/archives/archive_2057.asp.

23. Turner, "The Significance of the Frontier in American History."

24. Herbert Clark Hoover, "Principles and Ideals of the United States Government," speech, October, 22, 1928; transcript courtesy of the University of Virginia's Miller Center, http://millercenter.org/president/speeches/detail /6000.

Chapter 7

1. William Strauss and Neil Howe, *The Fourth Turning: An American Prophecy* (New York: Broadway Books, 1997), Kindle edition, Chapter 6, "First Turnings and Archetypes" subheading, 31st paragraph.
2. Frederick Douglass, "Self-Made Men," Frederick Douglass Heritage, 1871, http://www.frederick-douglass-heritage.org/self-made-men/.
3. Cat Stevens, "If You Want to Sing Out, Sing Out," A&M, 1971, lyrics available at http://www.azlyrics.com/lyrics/catstevens/ifyouwanttosingoutsingo ut.html.
4. "Follow Your Bliss," Joseph Campbell Foundation, accessed September 9, 2014, http://www.jcf.org/new/index.php?categoryid=31.
5. "1984" Television Commercial, Apple Inc. (first aired: December 31, 1983, KMVT) https://www.youtube.com/watch?v=axSnW-ygU5g, accessed February 22, 2014.
6. Neil Howe, interview with the author, September 24, 2012.
7. Rick Newman, "Why the Economy Is Addicted to Government Aid," *U.S. News & World Report,* August, 10, 2010, http://money.usnews.com/money /blogs/flowchart/2010/08/10/why-the-economy-is-addicted-to-govern ment-aid.
8. Chana Joffe-Walt, "Unfit for Work: The Startling Rise of Disability in America," National Public Radio, March 25, 2013, http://www.npr.org /2013/03/25/175293860/in-one-alabama-county-nearly-1-in-4-working -age-adults-is-on-disability.
9. Charles Murray, *American Exceptionalism: An Experiment in History* (Washington, DC: AEI Press, 2013), Kindle edition, Chapter 3, "American Traits" subsection, second paragraph.
10. Ibid., Chapter 2, "Exceptional Traits" subsection, fifth paragraph.
11. Milton and Rose Friedman, *Free to Choose: A Personal Statement* (Orlando, FL: Harcourt, 1980), Kindle edition, Chapter 1, "Cooperation through Voluntary Exchange" subsection, first paragraph. Leonard E. Read wrote the essay Friedman mentioned frequently, which was fully titled, "I, Pencil: My Family Tree as Told to Leonard E. Read" and originally appeared in a monthly journal called *The Freeman* in December 1958.
12. Jack Hough, "Five Big Investments You Don't Know You Have," *Wall Street Journal,* May 11, 2014, http://online.wsj.com/news/articles/SB1000142405 2702304431104579547702031198882.

Chapter 8

1. I learned later that the brown recluse spider is typically found in south-central states such as Kentucky, Arkansas and Louisiana and does not range as far north as New York. Thanks Omar! "Brown Recluse Spiders," University of California, Riverside, http://spiders.ucr.edu/brs.html, accessed October 26, 2014.

2. *U.S. Army Survival Manual (Reprint of the Department of the Army Field Manual, FM 21-76)*, US Department of Defense, 2012, Kindle edition, Chapter 1, "V—Value Living" subsection, first paragraph.

Chapter 9

1. Frederick Jackson Turner, "The Significance of the Frontier in American History," *Proceedings of the State Historical Society of Wisconsin*, December 14, 1893, http://xroads.virginia.edu/~HYPER/TURNER/.

2. Jessica Dickler, "Inside Sarah Palin's New Arizona Estate," CNNMoney, May 26, 2011, http://money.cnn.com/galleries/2011/real_estate/1105/gallery.sarah_palin_home/index.html.

3. Dwight Garner, "A New Breed of Hunter Shoots, Eats and Tells," *New York Times*, October 1, 2012, http://www.nytimes.com/2012/10/02/books/new-breed-of-hunter-shoots-eats-and-writes.html?_r=0.

4. Joseph Goldstein, "The New Age Cavemen and the City," *New York Times*, January 8, 2010, http://www.nytimes.com/2010/01/10/fashion/10caveman.html?pagewanted=all&_r=0. For more information on Durant, check out his Web site, www.huntergatherer.com.

5. Mandi Woodruff, "How This Family of Four Lives 'Off the Grid' in the Middle of the Desert," Yahoo Finance, January 15, 2014, http://finance.yahoo.com/news/family-life-off-the-grid-abe-connally-vela-creations-144054081.html. The Connallys' Web site is http://velacreations.com/. Their Flickr page is at http://www.flickr.com/photos/velacreations/.

6. Arthur Bradley, interview with the author, January 31, 2013.

7. Steve Hargreaves, "Woman Chases Oil Boom, Strikes It Big," CNNMoney, March 21, 2014, http://finance.yahoo.com/news/woman-chases-oil-boom-strikes-095900739.html.

8. Lewis Wilcox, James Christenson, Eliot Popko, and Johan Sargent, "Running on Fumes in North Dakota," *New York Times*, video short, January 13, 2014, http://www.nytimes.com/2014/01/14/opinion/running-on-fumes-in-north-dakota.html?_r=1.

9. Joel Kotkin and Mark Schill, "America's Next Decade," *Forbes*, September 4, 2013, http://www.forbes.com/special-report/2013/america-next-decade.html.

10. Raj Chetty, Nathaniel Hendren, Patrick Kline, Emmanuel Saez, and Nicholas Turner, "The Equality of Opportunity Project," Harvard University

and the University of California, Berkeley, accessed March 28, 2014, http://www.equality-of-opportunity.org/. This project ranks the 100 largest US cities in terms of upward mobility, or the ability of people to rise to a higher income group than they were born into. Those rankings are available at http://www.equality-of-opportunity.org/index.php/city-rankings/city-rankings-100.

11. Farnoosh Torabi, "Why I Choose to Be Rich and Homeless," Yahoo Finance, January 20, 2014, http://finance.yahoo.com/news/the-homeless-suitcase-entrepreneur-151051178.html.

12. William Strauss and Neil Howe, *The Fourth Turning: An American Prophecy* (New York: Broadway Books, 1997), Kindle edition, Chapter 6, eighth paragraph.

13. Neil Howe, interview with the author, September 24, 2012.

14. Rick Newman, "To Get Ahead, More Americans Must Do This One Thing," Yahoo Finance, January 21, 2014, http://finance.yahoo.com/news/to-get-ahead—more-americans-must-do-this-one-thing-193344201.html.

15. Josh Mandel, "Welders Make $150,000? Bring Back Shop Class," *Wall Street Journal,* August 21, 2014, http://online.wsj.com/news/article_email/SB10001424052702303663604579501801872226532-lMyQjAxMTA0MDIwMjEyNDIyWj.

16. David Brooks, "The American Precariat," *New York Times,* February 10, 2014, http://www.nytimes.com/2014/02/11/opinion/brooks-the-american-precariat.html?_r=0.

17. Sharon Jayson, "What's on Americans' Minds? Increasingly, 'Me,'" *USA Today,* July 10, 2012, http://usatoday30.usatoday.com/news/health/story/2012-07-10/individualist-language-in-books/56134152/1.

18. Brooks, "The American Precariat."

19. Turner, "The Significance of the Frontier in American History." See also Charles Murray, *American Exceptionalism: An Experiment in History* (Washington, DC: American Enterprise Institute, 2013), Kindle edition, Chapter 2, seventh paragraph.

Chapter 10

1. "James Truslow Adams Papers, 1918–1949," Columbia University Library Archival Collections, accessed November 3, 2014, http://www.columbia.edu/cu/lweb/archival/collections/ldpd_4078384/.

2. "Historical Census of Housing Tables," US Census Bureau, accessed November 3, 2014, http://www.census.gov/hhes/www/housing/census/historic/owner.html. The latest quarterly numbers are at http://www.census.gov/housing/hvs/data/histtabs.html.

3. Michael Lind, *Land of Promise: An Economic History of the United States* (New York: HarperCollins, 2012), 342, 388.

4. "Table 14: Quarterly Homeownership Rates for the U.S. and Regions: 1965 to Present," "Housing Vacancies and Homeownership," US Census Bureau, http://www.census.gov/housing/hvs/data/histtabs.html.

5. "The State of the Nation's Housing, 2013," Joint Center for Housing Studies of Harvard University, June 26, 2013, http://www.jchs.harvard.edu/sites /jchs.harvard.edu/files/son2013.pdf.

6. Mandi Woodruff, "1 in 4 Homeowners Regrets Buying a House," Yahoo Finance, April 29, 2014, http://finance.yahoo.com/news/homeowners -regrets-buying-a-house-redfin-163113390.html.

7. Rick Newman, "The 'Wealthy Poor' Replace the Middle Class," Yahoo Finance, March 21, 2014, http://finance.yahoo.com/blogs/the-exchange /how-to-be-poor—with-a-lot-160211942.html. Foreclosure figures were provided to the author by real estate research firm RealtyTrac.

8. Allen Salkin, "Annie Leibovitz Takes Steps to Regain Her Financial Footing," *New York Times*, December 10, 2009, http://www.nytimes.com /2009/12/11/arts/design/11leibovitz.html?ref=annieleibovitz.

9. Allen Salkin, "That Old Master? It's at the Pawnshop," *New York Times*, February 23, 2009, http://www.nytimes.com/2009/02/24/arts /design/24artloans.html.

10. Rick Newman, "How to Blow $300 Million," Yahoo Finance, May 30, 2013, http://finance.yahoo.com/blogs/the-exchange/blow-millions-215238921 .html.

11. Julie Creswell, "With Fortune Falling, a 1 Percent Divorce," *New York Times*, February 1, 2014, http://www.nytimes.com/2014/02/02/business/breakup -at-740-park-avenue.html.

12. See, for instance, Michael Greenstone and Adam Looney, "Thirteen Economic Facts about Social Mobility and the Role of Education," Hamilton Project, June 2013, http://www.hamiltonproject.org/papers/thirteen_economic_facts _social_mobility_education/?utm_source=The+Hamilton+Project&utm_ca mpaign=8fe05eed72-July_Newsletter7_29_2013&utm_medium=email& utm_term=0_f824d01d18-8fe05eed72-300393689.

13. Richard Reeves and Kerry Searle Grannis, "5 Strong Starts to Boost Social Mobility," Brookings Institution, January 13, 2014, http://www.brookings .edu/research/interactives/2014/strong-starts.

14. Charles Murray, "The New American Divide," *Wall Street Journal*, January 21, 2012, http://online.wsj.com/news/articles/SB10001424052970204301404 4577170733817181646.

15. Nassim Nicholas Taleb, *Antifragile: Things that Gain from Disorder* (New York: Random House, 2012), Kindle edition, Chapter 6, "What to Tell the Foreign Policy Makers" subsection, first paragraph.

16. Kip Hagopian and Lee Ohanian, "The Mismeasure of Inequality," Hoover Institution, August 1, 2012, http://www.hoover.org/research/mismeasure -inequality.

17. See, for instance, Erin Cammel, "The 'Growing' American Dream: An Analysis of Historic Trends in Housing," *Undergraduate Research Journal for the Human Sciences* 12 (2013), http://www.kon.org/urc/v12/cammel.html.

18. "Consumer Credit Outstanding," Federal Reserve, accessed February 26, 2014, http://www.federalreserve.gov/releases/g19/HIST/cc_hist_mt_levels.html.

19. "National Economic Accounts, Gross Domestic Product," Bureau of Economic Analysis, US Commerce Dept., accessed February 26, 2014, http://www.bea.gov/national/index.htm#gdp. US gross domestic product in 1968 was $943 billion. In 2013 it was $16.8 trillion.

20. "Quarterly Report on Household Debt and Credit," Federal Reserve Bank of New York, February 2014, http://www.newyorkfed.org/householdcredit/2013-q4/data/pdf/HHDC_2013Q4.pdf.

21. "Report to the Congress on Practices of the Consumer Credit Industry in Soliciting and Extending Credit and Their Effects on Consumer Debt and Insolvency," Board of Governors of the Federal Reserve System, June 2006, http://www.federalreserve.gov/boarddocs/rptcongress/bankruptcy/bankruptcybillstudy200606.pdf.

22. Jenna Goudreau, "Why This Millennial Quit His 6-Figure Job and Gave Away Most of His Possessions," *Business Insider,* January 31, 2014, http://www.businessinsider.com/minimalist-millennial-quit-job-and-shed-possessions-2014-1.

23. "Table 2.1. Personal Income and Its Disposition," "National Income and Product Accounts," Bureau of Economic Analysis, US Commerce Dept., August 28, 2014, http://www.bea.gov/iTable/iTable.cfm?ReqID=9&step=1#reqid=9&step=3&isuri=1&903=58. The savings rate is shown in line 35, "personal saving as a percentage of disposable personal income."

24. This information came from Stan Humphries, chief economist of real estate research site Zillow, in an interview with the author on May 22, 2013.

25. On their Web site, Millburn and Nicodemus list 21 ways to become a minimalist, one per day on a 21-day journey. Day 18 is devoted to the home: http://www.theminimalists.com/21days/day18/.

26. Morgan Korn, "How to Get More Out of Your Life by Doing Less," Yahoo Finance, April 1, 2014, http://finance.yahoo.com/blogs/daily-ticker/the-pursuit-of-less-152331662.html.

Chapter 11
1. Angie Drobnic Holan, "Top 16 Myths About the New Health Care Law," Politifact, September 25, 2013, http://www.politifact.com/georgia/article/2013/sep/25/top-16-myths-about-health-care-law/.

2. "Fuelish Pleasures," Snopes.com, March 28, 2011, http://www.snopes.com/autos/hazards/gasvapor.asp.

3. "Chain Email Says 11 States Have More People on Welfare than Employed," Politifact, accessed March 16, 2014, http://www.politifact.com/texas/state ments/2013/jan/11/chain-email/chain-email-says-11-states-have-more -people-welfar/.

4. "J.D. Hayworth Claims Massachusetts Ruling Opens the Door for Man-Horse Marriage," Politifact, accessed March 16, 2014, http://www .politifact.com/truth-o-meter/statements/2010/mar/18/jd-hayworth/jd -hayworth-claims-massachusetts-ruling-opens-door/.

5. Rick Newman, "Here's How Lousy Life Is in North Korea," *U.S. News & World Report*, April 12, 2013, http://www.usnews.com/news/blogs /rick-newman/2013/04/12/heres-how-lousy-life-is-in-north-korea.

6. Glenn Thrush, "Poll: 41 Percent Believe in Death Panels," *Politico*, September 14, 2009, http://www.politico.com/blogs/glennthrush/0909/Poll_41 _percent_believe_in_death_panels.html.

7. Dana Blanton, "Fox News Poll: 24 Percent Believe Obama Not Born in U.S.," Fox News, April 7, 2011, http://www.foxnews.com/politics/2011/04/07 /fox-news-poll-24-percent-believe-obama-born/.

8. "GOP Deeply Divided Over Climate Change," Pew Research Center for the People and the Press, November 1, 2013, http://www.people-press .org/2013/11/01/gop-deeply-divided-over-climate-change/; Drew DeSilver, "Chart of the Week: 63 Years of Global Climate Change," Pew Research Center for the People and the Press, January 31, 2014, http://www.pew research.org/fact-tank/2014/01/31/chart-of-the-week-a-half-century-of -global-climate-change/.

9. Rick Newman, "China Ain't All That: The U.S. Is Still Tops," Yahoo Finance, July 18, 2013, http://finance.yahoo.com/blogs/the-exchange/china -ain-t-u-still-tops-194311509.html.

10. Stephen Greenspan, "Why We Keep Falling for Financial Scams," *Wall Street Journal*, January 3, 2009, http://online.wsj.com/news/articles/SB123 093987596650197?mg=reno64-wsj.

11. Allie Bidwell, "American Students Fall in International Academic Tests, Chinese Lead the Pack," *U.S. News & World Report*, December 3, 2013, http://www.usnews.com/news/articles/2013/12/03/american-students -fall-in-international-academic-tests-chinese-lead-the-pack.

12. Carmen DeNavas-Walt, Bernadette D. Proctor, and Jessica C. Smith, "Income, Poverty, and Health Insurance Coverage in the United States: 2012," US Census Bureau, US Department of Commerce, September 2013, 33, https://www.census.gov/prod/2013pubs/p60-245.pdf.

13. "Income Distribution and Poverty," Organization for Economic Cooperation and Development, accessed March 14, 2014, http://stats.oecd.org /Index.aspx?DataSetCode=IDD.

14. "Country Comparison: Obesity—Adult Prevalence Rate," CIA *World Factbook*, accessed March 14, 2014, https://www.cia.gov/library/publications/the-world-factbook/rankorder/2228rank.html.

15. Paul Overberg and Meghan Hoyer, "Study: Despite Drop in Gun Crime, 56% Think It's Worse," *USA Today*, December 3, 2013, http://www.usatoday.com/story/news/nation/2013/05/07/gun-crime-drops-but-americans-think-its-worse/2139421/.

16. This quote is sometimes rendered as, "No one ever went broke underestimating the intelligence of the American people." The Web site *This Day in Quotes* claims the original, longer phrase appeared in a Mencken column published in the *Chicago Daily Tribune* on September 19, 1926: http://www.thisdayinquotes.com/search?q=mencken. It seems possible Mencken wrote the longer version and paraphrased it himself in later years.

17. Jason Brennan, *Libertarianism: What Everyone Needs to Know* (New York: Oxford University Press, 2012), Kindle edition, Chapter 4, Question 39, fourth paragraph.

18. Thomas E. Mann and Norman J. Ornstein, *It's Even Worse Than It Looks* (New York: Basic Books, 2012), 62.

19. Walter Isaacson, *Steve Jobs* (New York: Simon & Schuster, 2011), Kindle edition, Chapter 34, "Cancer" subsection.

20. See, for instance, Karen Reivich and Andrew Shatté, *The Resilience Factor* (New York: Broadway Books, 2002), 164.

21. "Washington's Farewell Address 1796," Yale Law School, accessed April 18, 2014, http://avalon.law.yale.edu/18th_century/washing.asp.

Chapter 12
1. "The Steve Jobs Legacy," Harvard Business School Working Knowledge, October 7, 2011, http://hbswk.hbs.edu/item/6848.html.

2. Walter Isaacson, "The Real Leadership Lessons of Steve Jobs," *Harvard Business Review*, April 2012, http://hbr.org/2012/04/the-real-leadership-lessons-of-steve-jobs/.

3. Walter Isaacson, *Steve Jobs* (New York: Simon & Schuster, 2011), 193–210.

4. Ibid., 303.

5. Ibid., 338.

6. Ibid., 5–10.

7. Ibid., 97.

8. Ibid., 98.

9. Ibid., 178.

10. Jonah Lehrer, "The Power Trip," *Wall Street Journal*, August 14, 2010, http://online.wsj.com/news/articles/SB10001424052748704407804575425561952689390.

11. Karen Reivich and Andrew Shatté, *The Resilience Factor* (New York: Broadway Books, 2002), 164.

12. "'You've got to find what you love,' Jobs says," *Stanford Report*, Stanford University, June 14, 2005, http://news.stanford.edu/news/2005/june15/jobs-061505.html.

13. "Wayne Gretzky Quotes," Brainyquote, accessed April 2, 2014, http://www.brainyquote.com/quotes/authors/w/wayne_gretzky.html.

Chapter 13

1. "Inventor of the Week: Mary-Claire King," Lemelson Foundation, October 1998, http://web.mit.edu/invent/iow/king.html.

2. Angelina Jolie, "My Medical Choice," *New York Times*, May 14, 2013, http://www.nytimes.com/2013/05/14/opinion/my-medical-choice.html.

3. Nancy Shute, "How Being Ignored Helped a Woman Discover the Breast Cancer Gene," National Public Radio, March 27, 2014, http://www.npr.org/blogs/health/2014/03/27/295270360/how-being-ignored-helped-a-woman-discover-the-breast-cancer-gene.

4. Alexis de Tocqueville, *Democracy in America*, vol. 2, trans. Henry Reeve, Kindle public domain edition, Chapter V, second paragraph.

5. Ibid., Chapter V, third paragraph.

6. Jay Yarow, "Google CEO Larry Page Spoke at TED, and Everyone Freaked Out Over His Ideas," *Business Insider*, March 19, 2014, http://www.businessinsider.com/larry-page-at-ted-2014-3#ixzz3BKUqZ4Py.

7. Richard P. Feynman, *The Pleasure of Finding Things Out: The Best Short Works of Richard P. Feynman* (Cambridge, MA: Basic Books, 2005), 112.

INDEX

14. Jon Clifton, "Americans Less Satisfied with Freedom," Gallup, July 1, 2014, http://www.gallup.com/poll/172019/americans-less-satisfied-freedom .aspx?utm_source=alert&utm_medium=email&utm_campaign=syndica tion&utm_content=morelink&utm_term=Americas%20-%20Government %20-%20USA.

15. Jeffrey Owen Jones, "The Man Who Wrote the Pledge of Allegiance," *Smithsonian*, November 2003, http://www.smithsonianmag.com/history/the -man-who-wrote-the-pledge-of-allegiance-93907224/.

Chapter 3

1. See, for instance, Michiko Kakutani, "The Attack Coming from Bytes, Not Bombs," *New York Times,* April 27, 2010, http://www.nytimes.com/2010 /04/27/books/27book.html?pagewanted=all&_r=0.

2. Daniel Bean, "Don't Risk Your Life to Save Your Smartphone," Yahoo Tech, July 8, 2014, https://www.yahoo.com/tech/dont-risk-your-life-to-save-your -smartphone-91043561164.html.

3. Alan Feuer, "The Preppers Next Door," *New York Times,* January 26, 2013, http://www.nytimes.com/2013/01/27/nyregion/the-doomsday-preppers -of-new-york.html?pagewanted=all&_r=0.

4. "Shelf Reliance," company profile, *Inc.,* accessed November 3, 2014, http:// www.inc.com/profile/shelf-reliance.

5. See a photo of Bradley and a brief biography here: http://www.nasa.gov /centers/Langley/news/researchernews/snapshot_ABradley.html.

6. The idea might sound crazy, but there's some scientific basis for the idea of a huge volcanic eruption that disrupts the entire earth's atmosphere, which has generated media coverage on programs such as the BBC/Discovery Channel special *Supervolcano.* There was also a 2008 issue of *Elements,* a journal published by the Geochemical Society, dedicated to the topic of supervolcanoes. See Erik Klemetti, "The Rise of a Supervolcano," *Wired,* October 4, 2013, http://www.wired.com/wiredscience/2013/10/the-rise-of-supervolcano/.

7. Sean Daly, "Fringe Fireman," *New York Post,* February 7, 2012, http://ny post.com/2012/02/07/fringe-fireman/.

8. "Emergency Preparedness—Seat of Your Pants NYC," Ad Council, accessed July 17, 2014, https://www.youtube.com/watch?v=wqrYO3_yQTw.

9. "Get Prepared: Gather Supplies," New York City Office of Emergency Management, accessed August 18, 2014, http://www.nyc.gov/html/oem/html /get_prepared/supplies.shtml.

Chapter 4

1. Ron Chernow, *Washington: A Life* (New York: Penguin Press, 2010), Kindle edition, Chapter 20, eighth paragraph.